Shipping Business Unwra͏͏

The shipping business is a lesser-known industry, but it is an extremely influential element in the global economy. This book provides a snapshot of the shipping business with micro-foundations from the perspectives of institutional and behavioural economics while uncovering hidden facts about the industry.

Rather than spending a great deal of time reading many books or consulting costly advisors about fundamental issues, readers can quickly and easily find core concepts examined from multiple perspectives. They will certainly enjoy the engaging, narrative-driven content and learn many surprising truths about this fascinating business.

Okan Duru is Assistant Professor of Maritime Studies at Nanyang Technological University, Singapore. His major research interests are maritime economics, computational intelligence for shipping economics, economic pluralism, maritime policies, shipping investment and finance. He received his PhD, on the Long-term Econometric Analysis of Dry Bulk Shipping, at the Graduate School of Maritime Sciences, Kobe University. He has published in various journals and conferences proceedings, in addition to reviewing and editing papers.

Routledge Maritime Masters

For more information about this series, please visit www.routledge.com/
Routledge-Maritime-Masters/book-series/RMM

Shipping Business Unwrapped
Illusion, Bias and Fallacy in the Shipping Business

Okan Duru

Routledge
Taylor & Francis Group
LONDON AND NEW YORK

First published 2019
by Routledge
2 Park Square, Milton Park, Abingdon, Oxon OX14 4RN

and by Routledge
711 Third Avenue, New York, NY 10017

Routledge is an imprint of the Taylor & Francis Group, an informa business

British Library Cataloguing-in-Publication Data
A catalogue record for this book is available from the British Library

Library of Congress Cataloging-in-Publication Data
Names: Duru, Okan, author.
Title: Shipping business unwrapped : illusion, bias and fallacy in the
shipping business / by Okan Duru.
Description: Abingdon, Oxon ; New York, NY : Routledge, 2019. |
Series: Routledge maritime masters ; 5 | Includes bibliographical references
and index.
Identifiers: LCCN 2018025589| ISBN 9781138292451 (hardback) |
ISBN 9781138292468 (pbk.) | ISBN 9781315231341 (ebook)
Subjects: LCSH: Shipping.
Classification: LCC HE571 .D87 2019 | DDC 388/.044--dc23
LC record available at https://lccn.loc.gov/2018025589

ISBN: 978-1-138-29245-1 (hbk)
ISBN: 978-1-138-29246-8 (pbk)
ISBN: 978-1-315-23134-1 (ebk)

Typeset in Times New Roman
by Taylor & Francis Books

MIX
Paper from
responsible sources
FSC   FSC® C013056
www.fsc.org

Printed and bound in Great Britain by
TJ International Ltd, Padstow, Cornwall

To Haluk, Kerem, and Kazue for their patience

Contents

Illustrations

Introduction

This state of things was brought about by the large OVER-PRODUCTION OF TONNAGE during the three previous years, fostered by RECKLESS CREDIT given by the BANKS and BUILDERS and over-speculation by the irresponsible and INEXPERIENCED SHIPOWNERS.[1]

E.A.V. Angier, *The Times*, London, January 7, 1885[2]

Most people take the shipping industry for granted. While consumers may know that many of their products come from overseas, they rarely stop to consider just how their purchases travel from a foreign country to the store's shelf. If they do think about oceangoing vessels, they often romanticize about the stories they know of shipowners and captains.

The reality is that modern shipping is an industrial operation comprising a complex web of logistics, thousands upon thousands of transactions, multi-million-dollar deals, and billions of dollars' worth of cargo. The finance functions supporting the maritime industry have also matured, with ships bought and sold as portfolio investments much like stock options, managed by corporate executives in suits, and subject to speculation with sophisticated financial instruments. Most importantly, the development of the maritime transportation and shipping business is one of the essential drivers of the globalization phenomenon.

Despite these advancements, the industry is still a long way from completely maturing. Due to the unique nature of shipping, the romantic sentiment attached to ships, the complexity of maritime law, unceasing shipboard operations, the frequent inaccessibility of the crews and vessels, and the long-standing traditions of the sea, the business has not experienced the same commercial and academic scrutiny as, say, the banking or manufacturing sectors. Many of the key elements that drive the industry are still little understood by practitioners, investors, and shipowners. Also, because professional management is a somewhat recent development, too many managers have too few resources to help them prepare for the challenges of managing a vessel, much less a fleet.

The classical view of economics assumed that people in a given profession are rational actors. Despite the challenges and critiques of other scholars, mainstream economists still maintain this view. They argue that while there may be some irrational decision-makers, such outliers will not determine the outcome of the whole and that the cumulative decisions of the marketplace will result in a rational outcome. Such people are assumed to be profit-maximizing agents who collect all available information, analyze it rationally, and make a decision unencumbered by emotions or other such limitations. In terms of the shipping industry, conventional economic publications usually focus on the supply-and-demand framework, the dynamics of the market, and models based on the theory of the rational actor.

Allow me to pose a simple but revealing question to challenge the bedrock of neoclassical economics: if people are genuinely rational actors as a collective whole, why does marketing exist? Moreover, why has it flourished? Why do inferior products sell well and their manufacturers thrive while the parent companies of superior products go bankrupt? Why do corporations spend millions upon millions of dollars on marketing campaigns and reap billions in return? In other words, why do TV commercials, social media branding and many other marketing tricks work?

Marketing is effective because it changes people's perceptions. It influences their spending habits in irrational ways. Were this true only of average consumers, we might not have experienced the national and even international market breakdowns that we have in the past. However, even the most educated and experienced people on the planet—those who should know better—succumb to their irrational natures. They, too, are vulnerable to making decisions based more on their emotions and perceptions than on cold, hard facts and concrete data. Edward Bernays (1955), known as the father of propaganda, demonstrated practically how marketing would change minds of crowds with his famous marketing campaign to promote female smoking using feminist symbols.

As more and more irrational behavior occurs and the debilitating effects are felt throughout the world economy, this classical assumption is increasingly being called into question. Whole global industries experience sharp declines and overnight collapses that take 'the experts' by surprise. The dramatic economic crises beginning in 2008 prompted a new wave of criticism and calls for a better understanding of how human decision-making affects the outcome of business and the global economy. Academics and the rest of the world were caught quite by surprise. After all, their complex financial models, derivative instruments, statistics, and predictive analytical tools completely failed them. Their carefully researched assumptions and forecasts were entirely swept away. The 'wizards' of the global economy were shown to be, at best, inept and, at worst, charlatans.

If the Great Recession taught us anything, it is that we still have a very long way to go in understanding the complicated relationship between collective market trends and individual human behavior. While financial analysts use predictive algorithms to forecast changes in markets, they may do so without ever verifying the reliability of the data they use for the calculation. Veteran practitioners in the field may believe they use only facts to inform their decisions yet be totally unaware of the illusory nature of the information they rely on. Newcomers to a market may follow the guidance of 'the experts,' ignorant of the fact that the experts adhere to practices that are no longer valid.

The shipping business is not immune to the influence of human nature in its operations, nor should it be isolated from the research currently being pursued in other fields. As in any industry, the decision-makers in shipping often revert to their unconscious instincts when making multimillion-dollar decisions, pursuing illusory information, entertaining obvious fallacies, falling prey to moral hazards, and succumbing to their own cognitive biases. The place to begin combating these natural tendencies is to recognize and understand them in the first place.

A broad theme of this book is that, ironically, believing in rational actors is profoundly irrational. Our collective personal, professional, and scholarly experiences refute the premise that we can continue to view the marketplace as being composed of rational actors and create models based on those assumptions. The truth is that it is quite rare for any individual to have access to perfect information, to be universally equipped to make the necessary calculations (e.g. Bayesian probabilities) and analyses, and to be trained to ignore their subconscious decision-making processes. To the best of my knowledge, this book is the first extensive introduction to the institutional and behavioral aspects of shipping business practice. While my studies and research stand up to academic rigor, I also recognize the practical knowledge that my friends and colleagues in shipping firms, financial institutions, brokerage houses, and consultancies need right now.

As such, I have written this book to explore the human side of shipping. The daily decisions that every shipping professional makes determines the short- and long-term success of their companies and affects others with whom they transact business. Many of those decisions are based on 'the way it's always been done' over generations. As such, many of the ideas and suggestions I present run counter to the prevailing advice and business norms. Although I have put a significant effort into making my arguments as clear as possible with examples and cases, there will be many areas of controversy and frank disagreement.

This book is not designed to be an in-depth discussion on all the different aspects of behavioral and institutional issues in shipping and potential countermeasures. Rather, it deals with high-level concepts, addresses the problems that arise from our human nature, and offers practical advice for avoiding the illusions, fallacies, and biases that have plagued the shipping industry for decades (if not centuries). I have drawn from the most recent research available and especially the emerging fields of heterodox economics and economic pluralism. In addition to the institutional and behavioral focus, some chapters will shed light on practical solutions and developments.

It is my hope that by demonstrating how our human nature affects our economic decisions in the shipping business, I will enable you to examine your actions more critically and use better judgment as well as providing the necessary awareness and the new conceptual apparatus to succeed in the shipping business.

Notes

1 This statement is what I call 'the shipping déjà vu.' If one had made the same statement in 2010, it would still have been such a fresh argument.
2 Also see the Angier brothers' *Freight and Steam Shipping Review* dated 1884, compiled in Angier (1920).

1 The fundamentals of shipping economics

Perfections, simplifications, and the big picture

*Neoclassical economics • Behavioral economics
Supply-demand framework • Seaborne trade
Shipping markets • Action-knowledge*

The shipping business falls under a particular branch of transportation economics and is a highly specialized field of study. Its technical context makes it highly sophisticated and complex. Newcomers to the industry must first understand the variety of ship types, the market, the applicable national and international legislation, charter parties, the terms and conditions of shipping contracts, and so on just to grasp the basics. It is a kind of entrance exam that eliminates the average person but attracts highly motivated people.

The fundamental economic framework of the shipping business is developed based on the neoclassical economics. The main instrument of this approach is the supply-demand framework: the balance of ships (supply) and cargo (demand). This framework is capable of explaining the broad phenomena and can assist in policymaking and strategy development; that is, the 'big picture.'

Imagine a masterpiece painted by a legendary artist. If I showed you the entire picture and asked you to copy it, it would probably be an impossible task. However, if I showed you how to paint like they did, the finer points of their brushwork techniques, how they mixed their paints, and so on, it would not be as difficult. Although you may not produce a perfect copy, you might do a decent job. If people were to see it from a distance, it might even seem good. However, the closer they looked, the more inconsistencies they would spot.

This is how it is with neoclassical economics. It can provide us an impression of the business and help us understand some of the common trends. It may be an imperfect perspective, but we can at least see the broader picture. Despite its advantages, though, such a framework is usually not practical for businesses. While such models are quite valuable to those who study the industry, there is an academic barrier between what we find and what is meaningful to people in everyday situations.

The behavioral economics of shipping may fill the gap between practical knowledge and academic theory. It serves as a checkpoint to help decision-makers see the illusory information, fallacies, and, most importantly, cognitive biases in the shipping business.

In the neoclassical economic model, humans are rational actors who collect all information and can distinguish between the signal (i.e. useful information) and the noise (i.e. meaningless oscillations). Of course, this is an oversimplification of actual human behavior.

We do have emotions, interests, a variety of personal characteristics, and even personal biases. Our biased nature seems helpful to survive in daily life. If we were actually rational actors gathering all relevant information, we would become paralyzed by a decision as simple as what to put in our shopping cart. We need our seemingly irrational intuition just for day-to-day survival. Our emotions are particularly valuable when we must make decisions in the face of risk and uncertainty. Professionals in the shipping business need to rely on their emotional intelligence to help them make day-to-day decisions. I am simply advocating that they need to recognize the drivers of such behavior and develop the appropriate measures to deal with them.

Before proceeding to the following chapters of this book, a quick review of the basic economics of shipping would be useful for both beginners and professionals. Therefore, this section will demonstrate the supply and demand framework in brief.

Dynamics of demand

The demand for shipping is simply defined as the amount of cargo that requires transportation. As a principle, it does not refer only to cargo in transit or already shipped. It also covers the 'agreed demand' (already negotiated and waiting to be shipped) as well as the 'prospective demand' (being negotiated but not yet finalized). As such, accurately calculating demand is difficult. However, we can estimate derived demand from certain leading indicators.

The fundamental measures used in the shipping industry are the distance navigated in miles and the volume of cargo transported in metric tons. Together, they form the ton-mile, the standard measure used in maritime transportation. The term 'seaborne trade volume' refers to the ton-mile rate of completed shipments in a given period. Although some regard it as measuring the demand for shipping, its precision is questionable at best. Whether shipped, in transit, or awaiting transport, demand as defined here is not helpful for decision-makers. Such a measure may be useful for predicting some future trends, but there are other, more predictive measures.

The major factors in shipping demand are world trade and the overall health of the global economy. The process that drives shipping demand begins at supermarkets, electronics stores, real estate offices, shopping malls, and so on; that is, consumer demand in the retail market. Rose George summarized the size of the maritime transportation industry in the title of her fascinating book *Ninety Percent of Everything* (2013). Much of the world population is unaware of how most of their goods, serving their daily needs, are made possible by this industry. Nevertheless, our purchasing trends directly result in higher or lower shipping activity.

Think about an automobile. Its steel structure depends on timely shipments of iron ore, coking coal, and steel plates as intermediary inputs. Its plastic components require petrochemicals, its interior section needs textile products, and its tires depend on rubber. The manufacture of just one car requires a massive yet organized transportation system.

Step by step, every consumption trend is supplied by shipping. The resulting seaborne trade volume is the outcome of completed shipping transactions. As such, it is more of a lagging indicator than one showing the current state of the market. Many people use seaborne trade volume as an indicator of shipping demand, but as I have shown, is it neither a useful nor a precise measure. It simply does not indicate true demand. In addition to the issue of time lag, there is also the problem of uncounted cargo sitting in warehouses, being held until the manufacturer receives an order or until the market price is just right. Moreover, there is the issue of mismatched supply and demand. Sometimes, there is more cargo to transport than there is cargo capacity. On the other hand, some ships cannot be matched to cargo and so sit idle, evidenced by the number of lay-ups. Therefore, the seaborne trade volume is never a perfect representative of the demand for shipping services.

It is an illusory measure because it is premised on the assumption of a mature market. In such a market, all ships and cargoes are in equilibrium— that is, there is an implicit assumption that the supply of carrying capacity is perfectly matched to the demand for it. Also, it assumes there is no lost time in searching and negotiating. For all these reasons, seaborne trade volume is useful for analyzing what happened in the past but rather difficult to use in predicting what will happen going forward. This particular challenge is discussed in the next chapter.

Dynamics of supply

The supply side of the shipping industry is defined as the shipping fleet available to transport cargoes. Like its demand counterpart, precise measurement of supply is an illusive goal. At times, it is virtually impossible.

The conventional approach to measuring supply is to take the existing fleet size of the industry, subtract existing lay-ups, and factor in a rough estimation of the 'slow steaming' effect.

Every ship is rated according to an optimal speed, which depends on its design and initial test conditions. During peak market conditions, companies tend to speed up operations and therefore increase the speed of their ships as well. During such conditions, the increased fuel costs are marginal compared to the higher earnings. But during poor market times, companies reduce speed slightly (slow steam) in order to save costs. Since it is relatively difficult to find profitable charter contracts in poor markets, there is no rush for ships.

How can we measure such variables? A ship's speed might be due to slow steaming, but what if reduction in speed was necessary because of the weather? Even if we did have information about all the technical, economic, and external conditions, could we still have any degree of confidence in how we measure supply? The ambiguity involved in measuring transportation capacity is amazing. For these reasons and more, nearly everyone has their own methods of estimating supply.

To find the size of the industry's fleet, begin with the fleet size of the last time period and subtract demolitions and idle ships (e.g. lay-ups, slow steaming, those in repair yards, etc.). These days, it is quite easy to find the scale of the active shipping fleet by using automatic identification system (AIS) data.

To arrive at the total volume of supply, we need to calculate the maximum carrying capacity for each ship in use as well as the required time for navigation, transportation, and cargo handling. Every ship has an average in-use period, usually assumed as 350 days a year. However, considering all information needed for this arithmetic, it is quite a puzzling calculation.

We also need to estimate the lifespan of each ship in the fleet. Plenty of them have been in operation for over 30 years. How much more use can be extracted before the ship has to be scrapped? The quality of shipbuilding and the operation of the ship itself play a big part in answering this question. Some ships age more rapidly than others. Some have more technical problems than others. We must also consider the quality of maintenance and repairs. Larger companies with sizeable fleets often keep their ships in better condition than their smaller competitors. All these factors come into play when calculating the supply of shipping economics.

When estimating the economic worth of a ship, there are external factors that also come into play, independent of the physical condition. For certain cargoes, some older ships may remain fully in use even though they have outlived their estimated lifespan. On the other hand, some younger ships are sold for scrap because of their residual value. When the price for iron ore and coking coal go up, manufacturers often turn to scrap metal as a cheap alternative. In times of economic downturn, some shipping companies often use the scrapyards as sources of much-needed capital. The problematic issue that arises with scrapping is whether or not the ship is actually scrapped. Some risk-takers see the value of a ship sold for scrap, buy her from the scrapyard, and put her back in operation. By the same token, some ships are contracted to be built yet never are. Cancellations, exit clauses, bankruptcies, and the like all affect whether or not a contract for construction of a vessel is actually seen through to completion.

While such declared transactional data (ships sold for scrap or contracted to be built) are usually included in estimating supply, we cannot be sure about its reliability. As you can see, the supply side of the shipping industry is just as difficult to calculate as the demand side.

Shipping markets

There are four main markets in the shipping business: the freight market, the new building market, the sale and purchase market, and the demolition or scrap market. In addition, there are other relatively small markets or sub-markets, such as marine insurance, repair and maintenance, ship supplies, etc. The nature of these sub-markets is somewhat different from that of the larger ones, making it difficult to classify them as economic markets per se. For the purposes of this book, we will limit our discussion to the four essential markets.

The **freight market** concerns prices for shipping services. In general, it usually drives the other markets. Any dramatic change in the freight market almost always spills over into the other markets quickly. For example, if freight rates were down and then recover, asset prices follow and demolition prices decline accordingly. In the neoclassical model we use here, the freight rate would be the equilibrium price between supply and demand. Theoretically, as the volume of supply or demand change, the equilibrium price changes correspondingly. Although the economic model explains the relationship, it is quite difficult to cover all aspects affecting supply and demand, as we have already noted. Using this classical framework requires us to assume a number of 'facts,' such as human beings are rational actors and mature markets lead to equilibrium prices.

In the freight market, shipbrokers play a critical role in matching ships and cargoes. For each transaction, or 'fixture,' two to three shipbrokers each collect a commission, usually 1.25% of the lump sum freight rate. This means around 2.50% to 3.75% of the total freight service goes to shipbrokers.

A somewhat recent development is that many professional shipbrokers provide not only the matching service but also consulting for ship-related investments as well as independent ship management services. The main benefits of what they sell, though, are their business networks and professional assessments of contracts as representatives of parties.

Returning to the general market, freight rates for different ship sizes naturally vary. To understand the overall trends in the business, we use freight indices aggregated from a number of trading routes and contracts. The Baltic Exchange is a well-known and globally accepted institution that publishes such indices for various ship types and tonnages. As such, its indices, such as the Baltic Dry Index, are widely used. (The motto of the Baltic Exchange is also a common slogan among shipbrokers: 'Our word is our bond.' However, the business practices of many opportunists in the freight market devalue this saying.) These indices are calculated by a group of panelists based on declared fixtures or trend basis estimations. As such, the quality of data is questionable, but it at least gives us an indication of the current state of the market.

Another major market in the shipping industry is the **sale and purchase market** (also referred to as the S&P market or the secondhand market). As is frequently said in the business, asset play is one of the major motives of the industry (for many, it is the sole objective). Therefore, in the S&P market, managing investment timing and shrewdly managing assets is crucial. Shipowners should simultaneously investigate opportunities in the freight market and S&P market to find a way to survive in this risky and volatile industry. S&P brokers are the intermediaries for the market, and their work is somewhat different from freight market brokers. In part because the value of a transaction is much more than that of a charter party and in part because ships are technical assets, the process of S&P always moves slowly.

The third major market is **the new building market**. In today's industry, shipyards have their own designs and optimize their production lines by building identical ships. Shipowners can select from a few designs and have limited options for modifying them.

In the last few decades, new building brokers have begun to help shipowners determine the right ship and shipyard for their new vessel. They rely on their experience and network connections with shipyards throughout the world. However, many shipowners still prefer to deal with the shipyards directly and manage the process on their own.

The fourth and last major market we will discuss is **the demolition or scrap market**; that is, the market for old ships. At the end of its useful life, every ship is broken down into its component parts and used in scrap-based steel production. As discussed earlier, there is no standard age for determining when to scrap a ship. The decision is based on the experience of the ship's owner, current market conditions, its physical condition, and other factors.

Breaking down a ship is generally a dirty business, including the risk of asbestos exposure. As such, there are a limited number of scrapyards. Some, though, have strict processes and observe safety and environmental concerns. Obviously, companies with strong green policies prefer these yards.

Models of shipping markets and the hidden forces behind our decisions

There is a strong academic emphasis on modeling shipping markets and predicting/estimating the dynamics of the business. Statistical methods, time series analyses, and econometrics are frequently used for testing models and finding the magnitude of factors within particular markets. Although a large volume of academic literature deals with modeling, it is still difficult to say that we have fully uncovered the big picture. Among the data limitations and assumptions I have addressed, there is one that has been scarcely addressed: irrationality.

Irrationality comprises our emotions, our bodies' neuroscience, our motives, individual incentives, our personalities and characteristics, and everything else that blends together to form our cognitive biases. As discussed, the classical economic model does not adequately account for our irrationality. That model is not wholly inferior, but it does need some adjustment to more accurately reflect the reality of what goes on in everyday business and even in our own minds.

Sections of our brain play a significant role in controlling how we collect and process information, as well as the decisions we execute based on that knowledge. The studies of neuroeconomics, neurofinance, and neuromarketing were all born from examining the intersection of neuroscience and the other fields, respectively. By the same token, the intersection of psychology and economics led to the study of behavioral economics.

Economists develop models from the application of knowledge; in other words, action-knowledge. Behavioral economics was, in part, the next step in creating an economic model that represented all the actors and influences in business. The so-called heterodox economics (or 'bad boys' economics') shed light on the shortcomings of the classical model of economics, effectively demolishing it as a stand-alone framework. While the classical model provided a good knowledge base for understanding the shipping industry, its time has passed. We must move on to a better way of understanding the market.

Human beings behave irrationally. We are blinded by our emotions, we believe in fallacies, we have beliefs we ascribe to, we have individual motives and incentives, and we are often misled. We cannot change this. However, we can mitigate this by understanding the hidden forces behind our decisions and equipping ourselves with tools and instruments to deal with them.

2 The story of the ton-mile

Can we really measure demand or supply in the shipping business?[1]

History of economics thought • Ton-mile metric
Supply-demand framework

The history of conventional economics and that of maritime economics as a branch of applied economics coincide in many facets of theoretical interpretation as well as practical use. Therefore, it is not surprising to notice that many leading economists studied maritime-related topics during their academic careers. Lincoln Paine, in his work *The Sea and Civilization* (2014), strikingly emphasizes that "all history is maritime history." Every aspect of our modern maritime economics theory is basically born out of conventional economic theory and its incubation nests. Bulk shipping economics broadly leads the research in maritime economics and is considered a frontier considering its history goes back much further than that of other segments, such as liner shipping. The current school of maritime economics is built on some fundamental hypotheses:

- Freight rate (bulk shipping) is settled in an environment led by supply of bulk shipping services (usually attributed as fleet capacity) and demand for bulk shipping services (usually attributed as seaborne trade volume).[2]
- Supply of shipping services is very inelastic[3] (difficult to build ships in the short run).
- Shipping markets are efficient, at least in the long run[4] (no room for price arbitrage).
- Bulk shipping markets are perfectly competitive[5] (so many players).
- Price in the shipping business is mean-reverting (freight market memory) and stationary random walk series with no predictability.[6]
- Period freight rate is the expectation of future spot rate (i.e. term structure).[7]

Despite their central role, the various hypotheses are accepted and rejected in different parts of the literature depending on the time period or the method used for testing procedures. Therefore, we cannot easily assume their generality and robustness. In addition, even the way we use statistical inference changes over time.[8]

The supply-demand framework also plays a central role in theoretical under-pinnings of maritime economics, in close connection with these hypotheses; and at some point, they are proof of each other. Although the supply-demand fra-mework is well established theoretically (theoretical-laboratory economics), measurement of real supply and demand is quite difficult in practice. The supply-demand framework was first developed by the so-called fathers of economics in an era of physical discovery boom, and the theory is very much inspired from its mechanical perspective. The emergence of Austrian, behavioral, and institu-tional schools of economics broadly relies on the gap between the mechanical narrative of economics and the economic phenomenon in practice.

In maritime economics, measurement of supply and demand for shipping services is established with the ton-mile metric. Two dimensions of shipping services are thought to be essential: the volume of cargo being carried (ton) and the distance sailed (nautical mile) for the shipment. The product of these dimensions (ton-mile) is globally assumed to be the scale of shipping services. In this chapter, the ton-mile approach is revisited and critically reviewed with its historical backings and the basis on which the theory is built.

Supply and demand for shipping services: measurement debate

Mainstream economics particularly emphasizes the supply-demand frame-work for pricing of products and services. Pricing shipping services (i.e. freight rate formation) is thought to be a typical example of the supply-demand-led Walrasian equilibrium mechanism including some negligible external factors such as politics and social setting (in most studies, it is either ignored or assumed limited) (see Walras, 1874). Based on this origin, supply-demand analysis is a key part of both academic and professional assessment of ship-ping markets. Before moving one step further, a comparative analysis of the shipping industry and other service industries would be timely and useful.

In the conventional service industry (e.g. restaurants, hotels), demand fac-tors are usually measurable and allow assessments in relation to the limited size of their markets. A restaurant in a city merely serves the population around the city, and short response times (customer visits, completion of ser-vice) enables the number of customers and the volume of required services to be counted. A hotel located in a metropolitan area is designed for guests vis-iting that particular city and local area, within relatively small boundaries. Data are readily available at any time. Most importantly, the number of cus-tomers that are declined or not serviced in a timely way (delayed) are known to key decision-makers, and this aids design and restructuring of facilities and capacity. For example, a customer waiting in a queue at a restaurant is explicitly known to managers. In modern restaurant chains, you may also find numerators which dynamically record requests and waiting times. Knowing the volume of both serviced and non-serviced customers is useful for future planning and pricing of services. The capacity of restaurants can also be calculated roughly based on service time, number of seats, etc.

On the other hand, the bulk shipping business is a complex one compared to other service industries. Similar to hotels and restaurants, the shipping service is a 'non-storable' and 'non-transferable' product. Shipping service capacity is available even when it is not used. A critical question here is how to measure supply or demand for shipping services. The 'ton-mile' metric has been used in measuring supply-demand for shipping services in the last century, and its origin actually goes back to railway transport.

History of the 'ton-mile' and its rationale

In the modern economics of maritime transport, shipping service is assumed to be measured via the ton-mile metric. The definition of ton-mile metric takes into account two major dimensions of shipping services: (1) size of cargo (ton) and (2) distance sailed (nautical mile). A century ago, shipping services were not specialized, and merchant ships were very similar to each other. Dry bulks were carried in bags while wet bulks (e.g. vegetable oils) were carried in barrels. However, the modern form of shipping is totally different from its ancestors. For understanding the logic behind the ton-mile metric, a historical review would be illuminating.

The term 'ton-mile' has been used for railway transport in the last couple of centuries. There is a vast number of publications referring to ton-mile metrics when dealing with the production of railway transport services. However, its use in maritime transport goes back to 1871. To the best of our knowledge, based on extensive search, Walter Carl Bergius, a naval architect, first utilized the ton-mile metric in relation to maritime transport in the *Journal of the Society for Arts* (1871). He wrote an article titled "On the commercial economy and performance of several types of merchant steamers on some of the principal lines of steam-ship traffic" in which he explicitly indicated the railway transport analogy:

> The performance of the five ships is given in carriage units, called "ton-miles," computed in an analogous sense to "train-mile" in railway terminology. A ton-mile is the performance accomplished in carrying one ton of deadweight for the distance of one nautical mile; therefore, if a ship carries 200 tons deadweight, besides her coal, upon load draught, and runs a distance of 35,000 nautical miles per annum, her total annual performance as a freight carrier is 35,000 × 200, equal to 7,000,000 ton-miles.
>
> (Bergius, 1871, p. 433)

Similar calculation for various carriers was presented in the article (see Figure 2.1).

Walter C. Bergius is an interesting figure in industrial history. His father-in-law, William Teacher, was the founder of Teacher Scotch Whiskey Distillery (still active and owned by Bean Suntory Co.), and his son, Walter McDonald Bergius, was the founding partner of Kelvin Marine Engines (still active and owned by

ANNUAL COST AND ANNUAL COMMERCIAL PERFORMANCE OF FIVE MERCHANT STEAMERS RECENTLY CONSTRUCTED

TYPE OF SHIP.	ANNUAL COST OF SHIPS.				ANNUAL COMMERCIAL PERFORMANCE OF SHIPS.			
	Interest, tear and wear, maintenance, and insurance accounts.	Coal and Engine Store Accounts.	Crew and Provision Accounts.	Total Annual Cost of Ships.	Dead-weight besides Coal.	Mileage per Year.	Commercial Performance per Year.	First Cost of Commercial Performance.
	£	£	£	£	Tons.	Nautical Miles.	Ton-miles.	Pence per ton-mile of Carriage.
1.-German Ocean Water Ballast Collier	3,100	540	1,350	4,990	1,000	38,000	38 millions	0.031d.
2.-Balstic Goods Carrier	4,500	2,450	1,850	8,800	1,000	37,000	38 „	0.057d.
3.-Home Trade Grain Carrier	1,500	520	1,250	3,270	350	38,000	13½ „	0.058d.
4.-Foreign Coasting Steamer	3,500	4,750	1,550	9,800	500	38,000	19 „	0.124d.
5.-North Atlantic Mail Steamer	18,000	8,400	1,300	34,700	1,200	42,000	50½ „	0.165d.

Figure 2.1 The first use of the ton-mile metric for shipping services by Walter C. Bergius (1871)

British Polar Engines Ltd.) He was born in Germany (1847) and worked for a shipyard in Kiel as well as engaging in physical and mathematical studies at the University of Kiel. Then, he moved to Edinburgh and naturalized in Scottish citizenship while teaching astronomy at the Anderson College of Glasgow. He was the first chairman of the British-German Astronomical Society. Later, he returned to the shipbuilding industry. He owned Walter C. Bergius & Co., Engineers and Naval Architects, Glasgow.[9]

There are some publications utilizing and emphasizing the approach in the last quarter of the 19th century. For example, Thomas F. Woodlock wrote a book titled *Ton-Mile Cost* (1899) and discussed this methodology in relation to railroad transport analysis. Although his book focuses on the railroad industry, the concept is discussed at a more general level in the introduction, and the author prefers the term 'transportation' rather than the more specific 'railroad transport.' *Ton-Mile Cost* appears to be the first publication on measuring in the transport service, and it is probably the only publication specifically dedicated to this topic in the history of mankind. The author included a very critical note, just after the introduction to the concept, on the first page of the first chapter (see Figure 2.2):

The passenger-mile is an abstraction, because it does not exist except as an arbitrary mental concept. The same is true of the ton-mile. Yet both

CHAPTER I. — THE UNIT OF TRANSPORTATION.

Transportation is the act of conveying something or some one over a certain distance. It is a combination of quantity and distance, and is therefore an abstraction which we may denote by the mathematical phrase:

$$\text{TRANSPORTATION} = \text{QUANTITY} \times \text{DISTANCE}.$$

Using the customary units of quantity and distance we have the units of the two kinds of transportation, thus:

$$\text{PASSENGER TRANSPORTATION} = \text{PASSENGER} \times \text{MILE}.$$
$$\text{FREIGHT TRANSPORTATION} = \text{TON} \times \text{MILE}.$$

Or, as we may for convenience denote them, "passenger-miles" and "ton-miles." These are the units of transportation , and no other units are possible, unless multiples of passengers or tons, or multiples of miles.

The passenger-mile is an abstraction, because it does not exist except as an arbitary mental concept. The same is true of the ton-mile. Yet both are real and true measures of transportation, whereas neither of the component parts is alone a measure.

Transportation is sold to the public practically in these units, although they are stated in a slightly different way, at least as far as freight is concerned. There may be laid down as general principles that—

Figure 2.2 Chapter I, the unit of transportation
Source: Woodlock (1899, p. 5)

are real and true measures of transportation, whereas neither of the component parts is alone a measure.

(Woodlock, 1899, p. 5)

The author clearly indicates that the ton-mile approach is just an abstraction, and it is absolutely not a complete measure of transport services. In addition to this limitation, the author mentions neither 'demand' nor 'supply' in the same context (these two terms are never used in the book). Thus, he does not associate the ton-mile metric with demand or supply.

In the 20th century, one of the pioneers of econometrics and also theory of maritime economics, Jan Tinbergen (First Nobel Laureate in Economics, 1969), utilized the ton-mile metric in his seminal work "Tonnage and Freight" (1934). In contrast to previous uses of the ton-mile metric, Tinbergen associated it with demand (i.e. demand index) while indicating the volume of tonnage and operating cost (i.e. coal price as marine bunker) as supply-side indicators (the "supply picture" in the original text). In various publications in the field since then, seaborne trade volume (ton-miles) has frequently been assumed as a demand indicator (e.g. Lun et al., 2010, p. 19). For example, in Eriksen's (1981) investigation of demand for bulk shipping, seaborne trade volume was again utilized as demand.

Challenges of the ton-mile metric

In theoretical economics, identical units are used for demand and supply so as to analyze prices balance or imbalance (i.e. equilibrium). Seaborne trade volume or, in other words, ton-mile (sum product) of 'materialized' (performed) shipments is preferred as a measure of demand rather than supply. In his supply-demand framework, Stopford (2009, p. 137) prefers the use of ton-mile metrics for both supply and demand sides. So, Stopford (2009) debiases the unit and balancing problem in the theoretical framework. The fundamental question is whether seaborne trade would be an indicator for demand or supply of shipping services. It is clear that the size of merchant shipping fleet is about the tonnage capacity for shipping while it is not the real size of shipping supply (deadweight tonnage, or DWT, vs. ton-mile).

Tinbergen (1934) also indicates the accuracy problem in demand analysis. The neoclassical approach assumes a unidirectional impact from demand to prices, and Tinbergen (1934) follows this principle while indicating that the contra-impact of price over the demand would be negligible or less than opposite. In other words, demand for shipping is fairly inelastic (demand-driven market).

There are two problems with the approach. First, seaborne trade (or ton-mile based on performed shipments) does not reflect shipments that are delayed or cancelled due to shortage of tonnage or unfeasible freight rates. There is no instrument to gauge its size and impact, and it is actually quite cyclical. When freight rates are taken over long-term average, shipowners usually fix their fleet easily and ships are very productive. On the other hand, cargo owners may have difficulty finding shipping space when the entire fleet is in a very productive and busy period. That will eventually cause rescheduling of shipments, delays, parcel size changes (getting larger with higher freight rates), and so on. During the opposite period of the market, freight rates are lower than long-term average, and the size of fleet is typically in oversupply cycle. In such circumstances, cargo owners will find tonnage easily, while shipowners will have difficulty employing their fleet. That eventually reduces productivity of the fleet (longer off-hire periods, slow steaming, layups). In the first example, seaborne trade is a more reliable indicator for supply (full capacity), while in the second example, it is better indicator of demand. So, it is quite difficult to have a common interpretation of seaborne trade volume. In between these opposite periods of the market, there will be various forms of demand-supply configurations, which further complicates things. The productivity level of a shipping fleet changes through time, and estimating its impact in the seaborne trade volume statistics is very uncertain.

The second problem is that the approach pretty much generalizes the demand for shipping, and it is implicitly assumed to be a static process. Even Tinbergen (1934), around a century ago, pointed out the various cargoes and tonnages, and today we also know that there are several cargoes and corresponding parcel size configurations. In addition to that, parcel sizes are not static, but they are dynamically settled in different global economy climates. For example, grain parcels may shift between Handymax (e.g. 45k DWT) and Panamax (e.g. 70k DWT) tonnages based on schedule and amount of trading activities. When demand for a cargo increases, cargo owners may merge parcels into a single Panamax shipment rather than double Handymax shipments in a time lag. With a growing global population and increasing consumption, there is also a long-term rising trend in parcel sizes. Last but not least, there are cargo exchanges between general cargoes/bulk cargoes and container shipping with the increasing capacity of bulk cargo containers (particularly tank containers).

Going back to its use by Bergius (1871), the ton-mile metric is explicitly a measure of transport, and attributing it as a measure of demand or supply always entails bias considering the above-mentioned features of the data. There is always a high positive correlation between dry bulk fleet capacity and dry bulk seaborne trade volume (e.g. over 0.85 for the last 30 years), and that causes a multicollinearity problem in econometric models with both demand and supply as independent variables. Measurement and analysis of shipping services has always been a great challenge in terms of collecting relevant data and modelling in econometrical instruments as well as interpreting the results. Predictability of the shipping markets is thought to be as low as when flipping a coin.

Adoption of the ton-mile metric in maritime economics

Considering the maritime economics literature, the most cited scholarly publication utilizing the ton-mile metric was written by Tinbergen (1934). It is obvious that Tinbergen's work has made a significant impact in the field, which did not exist beforehand. The persuasive power of Tinbergen is inevitable. He is known as one of the fathers of modern econometrics and was also the first Nobel Laureate (originally Bank of Sweden Prize in Economics). If we review a little bit of the background of early developments in economics, it is no secret that the age of Tinbergen was reliant on transfer of ideas from developments in physics. Beginning with the first quarter of the 1900s, the physical metaphor and the idea of explaining economic phenomenon with strict and abstract representations have grown dramatically (Bouchaud, 2008; Stanley et al., 2001). A unique assumption of this approach is the measurability of economic actions. So, the econometric approach requires the measurement of major components including supply and demand. Therefore, the ton-mile metric is a solution to the measurement problem in the shipping services.

In subsequent years, the vast majority of the literature has adopted Tinbergen's approach, though a number of scholars prefer a much more neutral position, such as that of Metaxas (1972). Metaxas (1972, p. 274) states that "the tramp freight market mechanism is not characterised by a stable equilibrium; demand is not always equal to the supply of tramp shipping tonnage at a price at which only normal profits are made." Thus, he also underlines the lack of real equilibrium in the market. Metaxas (1972) does not frame the shipping demand in the context of ton-mile measurement, but the weight of cargo (metric tons) transported by ships is investigated.

The ton-mile approach is reinforced by one of his colleagues and another Nobel Laureate, Tjalling C. Koopmans (1939), for tanker freight rates. Koopmans also clearly defines the ton-mile metric as a measure of both shipping supply and demand.

In Charemza and Gronicki (1981) and Beenstock and Vergottis (1993, p. 17), the demand for dry cargo freight is represented by ton-mile measurement. Charemza and Gronicki (1981) utilize an indirect approach while still following the ton-mile approach. In the theoretical analysis of Tvedt (2003, p. 343), the ton-mile metric plays an integral role again as a demand indicator. Glen and Martin (2002) also assume the association between the ton-mile metric and demand as opposed to supply or both.

Duru and Yoshida (2011) developed the Beenstock-Vergottis model with life expectancy theory while implicitly assuming the seaborne trade volume (again ton-mile) as the demand for shipping services.

Considering the acceptance of the theory and use of the ton-mile metric, it has become much more difficult to object to it and revisit its weaknesses. The majority of past and ongoing research in maritime economics implicitly or explicitly assumes the ton-mile metric as an indicator of demand in various ship types (also TEU-mile in container shipping). On the other hand, the real explanatory power of seaborne trade is very low since the seaborne trade volume for various cargoes has had a steadily increasing trend with no significant decline except for years when there was a market collapse (e.g. 2008) (Figure 2.3).

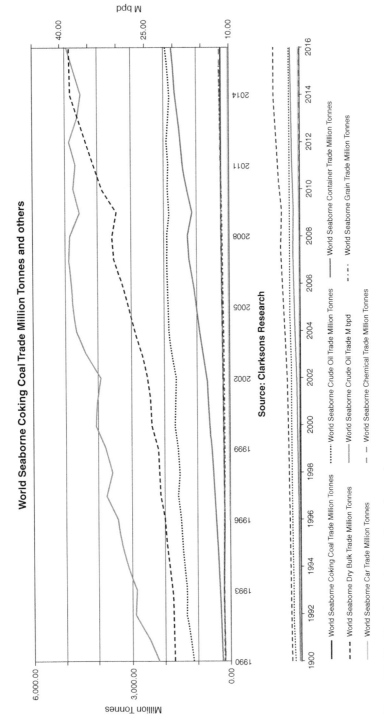

Figure 2.3 World seaborne trade volume for various cargoes

It is common to find a high level of correlation between long-term data sets since many of them are either positively or negatively trended. In a recent study, Munshi (2016) presented such spurious associations when proper data handling procedures are not followed.

There is another critical reason for use of the ton-mile metric. Econometric studies in maritime economics (also economics in general) are usually designed to observe relationships between variables (e.g. elasticities) in historical data. The predictive power of those models is never tested and presented in the current literature. The unique validation process for predictive power is the post-sample test of predictions generated by proposed models. The post-sample test of predictive properties of econometric models tends to be ignored, and therefore the gap between statistical significance in past data and practical impact in real data is always left undisclosed in modelling shipping markets. The ton-mile metric (seaborne trade volume) is one example of the problems of such inconsistencies.

***

Taking account of the inadequacy of supply-demand measurement instruments, utilizing the neoclassical framework has both theoretical and practical challenges. It is obviously not straightforward to employ seaborne trade as the volume of demand or supply since it is not technically a complete representation of either variable. Seaborne trade volume (ton-mile) may be a good predictor of demand at recession (oversupply, full utilization of shipments) or a good predictor of supply at upturn (undersupply, full utilization of fleet). But in both cases, various classifications of vessels and their cargo raise questions about the use of the ton-mile metric as a variable in conventional econometric analysis. Considering the changes in econometric models over time, there is potential for data omissions and/or invalidity of the econometric approach. Seaborne trade volume is still a good measure of activity level in the industry without attributing it to either demand or supply.

Notes

1 An earlier version of this chapter appeared in an academic paper (Duru, 2017).
2 For example, Stopford (2009).
3 Stopford (2009) and Lun et al. (2010), among others.
4 See Glen (1997); Adland and Koekebakker (2004); Adland and Strandenes (2006).
5 For liner shipping markets, several scholars indicate the weakness of market competition and existence of oligopoly; for example, Sys (2009) and Fox (1994).
6 At least nonlinear stationary (Koekebakker et al., 2006).
7 See Koekebakker and Ådland (2004) and Veenstra (1999), among others.
8 The American Statistical Association (ASA) recently published a statement on issues with the conventional use of statistical significance (Wasserstein and Lazar, 2016). A group of econometricians have redefined the use of the p-value (Benjamin et al., 2018).
9 For details of his life story, see *Jahrbuch der Schiffbautechnischen Gesellschaft: Band 11*, Springer.

3 Ships vs. assets
Fleet vs. portfolio

Shipping investor • "This time it's different"
Euphoria • Chicken's inductive reasoning
Fear and greed • Amygdala hijack • Market for lemons

There are fundamentally two kinds of investors in shipping: flag wavers and asset managers. The relationship between ships and their owners affect their future in the business. Some shipowners prefer to be quite attached to their ships, going so far as bestowing to them the names of their mothers, spouses, or other relatives. Even professional hedge fund managers like to think that they are the "shipping man" right out of Matthew McCleery's novel (2011). It is common to see this much meaning and emotion invested in being a shipowner.

We attach such significance to owning merchant ships because of how important the oceans have been in human history. Naval fleets have determined the course of nations and the rise and fall of empires. There is always an element of danger: despite advancements in technology and ships equipped with state-of-the-art technology, vessels litter the seafloor. Moreover, the lure of the unknown still entices us: we know more about our solar system than we do about the ocean. Being the owner of a ship taps into every culture's deep-seated awe of the sea. It is no surprise, then, that such inherent meaning affects how we look at ships. In any selling, buying, or building decisions, these emotions come into play.

The business of ship-owning, however, revolves around two main functions: asset management (S&P decisions) and asset operation. Historically, buying and selling vessels generates more profit than operating them. A newly built ship can lose 50% of her value in just a few months; but in the same span of time, she can also boost her value by the same amount. Fortunes have been made (and lost) timing the market.

The critical question, when trying to avoid those losses or seize those gains, is whether it takes luck or skill to do so? Luck certainly plays a factor. Unexpected events such as war, economic depression, or natural disasters affect ship operations and the overall market. However, the frequency of such occurrences and ships' relative exposure to such events are not as great as some people might think. In short, business skill and intelligence play the biggest role in success or failure.

The real challenge is minimizing our own emotions. Words impact strongly on how we perceive situations and, therefore, what we decide. The very term 'shipowner' has a strong emotional background embedded in its meaning. Instead, we could use the term 'shipping investor,' which focuses on the financial context.

When freight rates are high and everything is going well, we are happy (even euphoric). Making the decision to sell a ship is a difficult task in any case, but how much more difficult is it when it is hard to explain your rational decision to your emotionally attached shipping colleagues?

In the economic bubble of 2007, the order book volume (i.e. vessels contracted to be built) reached a historical high despite historically high costs. The price elasticity of contracting volume (i.e. the willingness to pay and purchase) also reached a historical peak. In practical terms, shipowners were spending money as if they were shopping for luxury brands on Fifth Avenue, New York.

To truly prosper in the shipping business, you have to learn an important lesson. A ship is not a toy. It is not a little pet to call by a cute name. It is not a source of enjoyment. It is merely an asset that transports cargo from one place to another.

In behavioral economics, the impact of ownership is called the 'endowment effect.' This is where we lose our ability to perceive things at their true worth. Instead, we overvalue our assets, whether we have already purchased them or intend to do so. Once we unconsciously create the emotional link, we often lose our critical judgment. Our asset management and investment performance skills follow accordingly.

There is also one more factor. It's called 'chicken's inductive reasoning' or 'Bertrand Russell's chicken.' Imagine a chicken newly arrived at a farm. The farmer feeds her every day. On the first day, the chicken is skeptical and worries about the farmer turning her into dinner. On the second day when the farmer feeds her and leaves her alone again, she worries a little less. As the days go by and the farmer does nothing but feed and care for the chicken, she finally becomes confident that the farmer has no bad intentions. He will feed her forever. But everyone on the outside knows that the farmer really has only one intention: chicken dinner (Russell, 2001).

Do you see any difference between this story and how people act in market bubbles? When the freight market is recovering, many people are skeptical: is this a real recovery or not? The higher that freight rates climb, though, the more confident shipowners are about the future: "This time it's different!" They believe the market will feed them forever; there is no reason to plan for a market exit or to consider reducing asset investment. Despite the high price they could get for their ship, they see no reason to sell, now or ever. They are irrationally exuberant.

The term 'historical peak' is actually very illusory. According to centuries' worth of data (from sources such as the Phelps Brown consumer index;

Phelps Brown and Hopkins, 1962), prices have a natural cycle as well as inflation. For instance, in the shipping industry, freight rates began to decline with the end of the Napoleonic Wars and continued to decline until World War I. Famous economic historians such as Douglass North (1958) investigated the reason behind the decline. He concluded that technological improvements made shipping easier. Others, myself included, point to the collapse of the British Navigation Acts, a kind of shipping cartel (Duru, 2012).

Recent history has conditioned many people to expect the average freight rate to continue to rise in the long term. Therefore, we expect occasional historical peaks. If you look at freight rates over the last half-century, you will notice that the magnitude of the cycles as well as the level of freight rates are growing. The costs of shipping and the demand for quality (or perception of quality) increase day by day. Freight rates are affected by such long-term factors as well.

The name of the game is good asset management. The motto of owning a ship is, 'Every entrance has an exit.' Once you purchase a ship, you should immediately begin to think about when to sell it. Regardless of your emotional attachment and the perceived market peak, you should never lose sight of the opportunity to sell your vessel. That is, unless you hedge your long-term risk (usually with a long-term time charter contract).

Market for lemons and ships

Today, we prefer the term 'shipping asset' to just ships or vessels when we refer to a sale. As I said earlier, I advocate that shipowners think of themselves as shipping investors. This redirects the focus away from being a captain sailing on the seas to the financial aspects of getting a return on a financial investment. Shipowners can still enjoy the feelings that come with being a shipowner, but as a result—not as a reason in itself.

Seen through the lens of a financial asset, a ship is like a stock that we follow on a stock exchange. Depending on the economy, we need to push the buy or sell button at the right time. There are many similarities between the two assets. There are bubbles, irrational exuberance, overconfidence, market collapses, and the wave-shaped peaks with gradually climbing rates followed by sharp declines. When you look at historical freight rates, notice that the cycles are never symmetrical. The left side always looks like gradually sloping valleys; the right side (once the euphoria is gone) always looks sharp, like the sheer side of a mountain.

I posit that this reflects the greed and fear cycle. Greed is what takes us to the top of the market. Fear is what we face when we have a fleet of ships, we have already negotiated to build more, we have traded in the spot market, and then suddenly the market collapses. It's what we would feel if we just finished eating a fine meal at a very expensive restaurant and then discovered that we had forgotten our wallet at home.

Greed and fear are two of the most popular topics in neuroeconomics. The amygdala, part of the neural system found at the base of the brain, governs most of our emotional responses. Such emotions can affect or even determine our reactions to certain situations (aka an amygdala hijack; Goleman, 1998). If you want to survive and thrive in the shipping industry, you need to understand how your emotional center works and affects your decision-making abilities.

Let's return to our analogy of shipping assets and the stock market. We sometimes react quickly to new information, such as a political declaration or a change in a central bank's interest policy. Since liquidity is usually high, we can quickly buy or sell.

The S&P process of a shipping asset takes time. If you want to purchase a secondhand ship, you must first assess its condition. Like Akerlof's (1978) "market for lemons," it is difficult to properly see its condition from the outside, beyond its size and number of cargo holds, without an expert. The ship must be berthed at a port, you have to find a person with reliable expertise to conduct a pre-purchase survey and coordinate their time, and only then—should everything go well—can you proceed to purchase it. This usually takes around a few months for the average shipowner. Because of how involved a process this is, it is difficult to time the market. By the time the transaction is completed, the edge of the crash may have passed or the window of opportunity closed.

Those who think they can catch the right time wind up with a massive long-term headache. Don't you think it would be easier and more practical to have a short-term headache by studying the nature of cycles beforehand and avoiding these types of mistakes?

Portfolio

In finance, the term 'portfolio' refers to a bundle of assets. It is commonly referenced when dealing with risk management. A portfolio is designed to include a variety of stocks with different risk characteristics that, in turn, distributes risk across the assets.

Likewise, a bundle of ships, or a fleet, is also a type of portfolio. Each company has a portfolio of ships with a variety of sizes, ages, and types. It is more common for companies to register their ships in different countries (i.e. flag of convenience) to benefit from lower taxes as well as creating a legal screen with a local registered company (a company for each ship). This helps to distribute the legal risk should one ship be caught in a legal dispute. A bareboat charter party or a ship management contract ensures the legal basis for transferring management to the principle company (i.e. group company).

A shipping portfolio is expected to cover a variety of ships with different long-term objectives and risk estimations. According to the unadjusted asset play strategy, a company's entire fleet should be sold before a market crash, but it is not a good idea to exit the market completely. The reason is customer loyalty. If you want to make a profitable and sustainable business in the shipping industry, you should have strong long-term ties with your charterers.

Sometimes you earn a lot, sometimes you lose a little, but all in all charterers value a good partner to help share the risk and grow together. In the Japanese shipping industry, this relationship has the highest priority. From a commonsense perspective, what customer would want to work with a shipowner who has a reputation for asset play and sudden exits from the market?

You should never lose your focus on the opportunity to sell your assets, but neither should you risk your long-term reputation. A shipping investor needs portfolio management that optimizes asset management while allowing for a stable business reputation.

There are many kinds of portfolio management styles in the shipping business. The shipping pool strategy is a popular method with big shipping companies. A shipping pool may consist of ships of similar size and type; for example, the LR2 pool of a product carrier. You may even charter out the pool rather than individual vessels. A ship in the pool navigates all around the world; they can reach any port based on the charterer's intention.

Another concern in managing a shipping portfolio is the average age of the fleet. For many charterers, the age of a ship is critical for the safe and straightforward transport of cargoes. Therefore, many shipping investors set an average age for the fleet and endeavor to keep this threshold as low as possible. Without considering the other factors in play, it may seem easy to manage. When doing so, you should match the decision to sell an asset with market conditions. When a ship passes over the age threshold, it may not be the best time for a sale in terms of the market and vice versa. It is a kind of optimization problem from an engineering standpoint and an econometric analysis from the economist's standpoint. When it comes to shipping, it isn't easy to kill two birds with one stone.

Non-asset-based investors

Shipping investors do not necessarily have to be shipowners. If you have strong ties with exclusive charterers and if you can gain high profits, above the market norm, you may prefer to play arbitrage. In this non-asset-based form of investing, you gather ships with time charter contracts and then trade them for your exclusive charterers' needs. There are a significant number of companies that can benefit from non-asset investment, and the opportunity of asset play is excluded. While this reduces your business risk, it also limits your potential opportunities.

4 Garbage in, gospel out

Fallacy and freakonomics of shipping statistics

Data quality ● *Shipping market data*
Self-serving bias ● *Illusory calculations*
Misleading statistics

All maritime data that we have is wrong!
An anonymous maritime research professional

Several institutions collect statistics on maritime transport. Shipping market reports can be purchased at reasonable prices, or you may even find sources of market data free of charge. Most of these reports provide spreadsheets of the data and perhaps some useful diagrams. However, to derive knowledge from them and answer your real questions will require a lot of effort on your part or outsourcing of the work to a consultancy. Creating knowledge in the shipping business is not as easy as some think. Doing so requires not only the right quality data but also a wider perspective, including economic history, market psychology, the global economic climate, and even political trends.

For any kind of proper analysis, we need the relevant information as well as the underlying knowledge. When we use any kind of data, we implicitly assume that it fits our objective, is qualified, is error-free, and has been methodically collected. The integrity of our information sources substantially affects the reliability of the knowledge we create from it. If we use bad data, we will have flawed conclusions. In other words, 'garbage in, gospel out.' Because multimillion-dollar decisions will be made based on the data, we must be diligent to ensure its quality as well as the validity of our results.

The integrity of the information supplier is not enough to validate the data. For example, a data series may illustrate monthly averages of a measurable phenomenon. You may know that the supplier is honest, presenting the real and unadjusted average values of the data. You have no doubt about its quality. However, an important thing you also need to know is the frequency of the data and its outliers. If you don't have all the detailed data used to calculate the monthly averages, you cannot investigate the frequency or the outlier effects.

There are standard reports as well as curated (and usually expensive) reports available. Standard reports rarely do more than give us a snapshot of the market—the same kind of conclusions we can derive on our own from free data sources, presentation handouts, trade journals, and so on. Curated reports tell us much more. The best method to arrive at the most reliable conclusions, though, is to collect raw data, develop your own analytical skills, and derive information yourself. You may have some headaches getting there, but that is nothing compared to the headache of being in the wrong place when the market crashes. If you are not going to analyze the data yourself, then at least hire an experienced company or analyst who can provide true consulting—not just one who can graph the data and let you draw your own conclusions.

Fixtures

As I pointed out earlier, we use the term 'fixture' in the shipping industry to refer to a shipping transaction (i.e. charter party agreement). One of the major components of shipping market reports is usually the list of fixtures. A fixture tells you which ship is fixed (chartered) for what type and tonnage of cargo, on which route, to whom, and the freight rate (plus some other technical points). You can learn about common tonnages, trending cargoes, the current level of freight rates, and potential charterers all from a single report.

When you look these data, sometimes you will see the conventional mark 'n/a' to indicate that data is not applicable, especially regarding the identity of the charterer. If you were to ask why the data are not applicable, you would receive a number of answers from different perspectives. Some parties may want to remain anonymous to avoid complaints. Also, some countries deny passage to ships containing cargoes from certain other countries (as in the Arab-Israeli dispute, for example).

Also, I question the reliability of these data. Without revealing charterers and ships, some parties can manipulate fixtures to mislead others who depend on the data (e.g. charterers). Since most of the suppliers of these data serve as intermediaries (i.e. shipping brokers), high freight rates—or at least the perception of high rates—may artificially inflate the market. Fixtures are the result of negotiations. If one side in the negotiation perceives that the market price for freight rates is higher than they actually are, this would affect their strategy. The process for arriving at the negotiated rate can begin at the opposite end, going from result (the fixture price) to reason (the market rate) instead of the other way around.

By inflating the freight rate, the two sides of the table have a reference or anchor point. In behavioral economics, the anchoring effect has been thoroughly discussed. The basic principle behind the theory is that people tend to make their estimations based on recognized data. In the above scenario, when approaching a contract negotiation, a charterer would consider as a starting point the current level of freight rates as reported in the fixtures data.

To address another data-related problem, let's talk about the basics of exchanging information. Imagine you are watching the news on TV. There are two filters at work: the intentional filter of the information source (i.e. the TV channel) and your own subconscious filter. You cannot control the flow, format, or content of your selected channel of information. Once you turn on the TV, the information simply begins to flow. However, you do have a choice about what information you allow past your second filter. The better able you are to filter out the irrelevant data (the noise) from your subconscious and keep only the relevant data (the signal), the more you can walk away with just the information you need. The same is true when examining data in the shipping industry: you cannot control the format and content of the data you receive, but you can train yourself to separate the signal from the noise.

Speaking about the reliability of data, let's talk about what I call 'pink adjustments.' This is when a party reports just a segment of the charter data instead of all of it. Allow me to demonstrate why this can be so misleading to those who rely on shipping data to gauge the market.

Say I have a list of ten charter contracts and their corresponding daily freight rates (the time charter equivalent, TCE, per day basis), as follows:

USD 13,000	USD 14,500
USD 13,500	USD 14,500
USD 13,500	USD 15,000
USD 14,000	USD 15,000
USD 14,000	USD 19,000

The simple averages of the left and right columns are USD 13,600 and USD 15,600, respectively. That is a difference of USD 2,000 per day. If we look at the medians (USD 13,500 and USD 15,000), the difference is USD 1,500. When working with averages, we should consider the impact of the freight rate of USD 19,000, an outlier that is probably not representative of the market.

With some simple arithmetic, we can find big differences between the columns and the data as a whole. The actual simple average of the entire data is USD 14,600 and the median is USD 14,250. With pink adjustments, I could report just one column or the other. One would have an incentive to skew the data in one's own favor. This is true not only for freight rates but for other types of fixtures as well, such as S&P and demolition fixtures. It is very common that the price of a recently sold ship is reported differently than the actual contract price. Having the knowledge of fixtures does not create a competitive advantage. You still need some exclusive knowledge; that is, the information not shared in these reports.

New building contracts

In the new building section of shipping reports, you can usually find a list of new building contracts fixed during the reporting period, similar to the fixtures in the freight market. It includes the names of the ship-owner and shipyard, the type and tonnage of the prospective ship, and its contracted price. At first glance, the data may seem intact, leading us to believe the report does its job. However, our work is not finished yet. To truly understand, we must examine the nature of new building contracts.

A new building contract mainly includes the technical particulars of a proposed design, the fiscal terms for payments, and the clauses around the failure of either party. (You can find a sample of such a contract.) Ostensibly, the purpose of a new building contract is simply to agree to deliver a shipping asset at a certain time. Since the shipyard probably has a queue of shipbuilding contracts, most shipowners will have to wait for a period of time. In truth, a new building contract has many more meanings than that.

There are other reasons for, and functions of, a new building contract. First of all, we should note that a new building contract can be cancelled. Sometimes this incurs a cancellation fee, but some contracts offer enough flexibility that this does not happen. For example, Chinese shipyards—backed by the Bank of China—offered very flexible contract terms in order to compete with South Korean and Japanese competitors during the historical upturn (2007–2008). As such, we cannot know with any degree of confidence whether a new building contract will actually result in delivery.

A new building contract is not necessarily a binding agreement for a shipowner. As such, some shipowners use these agreements as tools to achieve other objectives. For example, a publicly traded company may sign a new building contract to make it more attractive to investors. Such a contract can be taken as a signal of expansion, thereby raising market traders' expectations about the company and resulting in higher stock prices. Normally, a shipowner would want to find the cheapest ship available, but in these cases, we observe the same parties contracting shipyards for more expensive ships, which would mean acquiring a higher-value asset. Basically, it's engineering the stock price.

New building contracts also contribute to the brand value and publicity of the company. The name of the company is mentioned on these lists (allowing the owners to feel a certain amount of pride, or as I like to call it, the 'king of the seas' factor). Again, this is using the agreement as a kind of marketing instrument to portray the image of a growing shipping company.

Investment appraisal

A shipping investment needs to be examined against the long-term estimations from several data sources. At the end of the day, we want to know what the estimated return on equity is for the proposed project.

The calculation for such is something like the following:

Operating income (time charter equivalent basis, or TCE)
- Operating expenses, or OPEX (fixed costs, including wages)
- Capital expenses, or CAPEX (loan amortization, including interest and principal payments)

= Earnings before tax and depreciation, or EBTD

Each of these items has prior calculations and estimations. Most people are used to the more common term EBITDA (earnings before interest, taxes, depreciation, and amortization). EBTD excludes capital costs but still includes taxes and depreciation. However, I am unaware of any shipowners paying taxes elsewhere. The shipping business is mostly an offshore business, usually with ship companies registered in lesser-known cities and with bank accounts in another country. 'Flagging out' was a popular trend in the second half of the 20th century, where a company would register a flag of convenience (FOC) company. FOC-friendly countries usually do not require any significant amount of tax. They simply collect some fees and some paperwork. Some of these countries even follow the industry, revising their legal requirements in response to industry changes.

Another part of the equation is depreciation, something particularly important for GAAP rules (Generally Accepted Accounting Principles). In practicality, we just need the purchase price and the estimated residual (scrap) price at a certain age of ship (end of economic operating period). Every investment appraisal needs a time horizon to simplify calculations, even though you probably will not follow it due to the unpredictable nature of the market. At the beginning of the proposed time period, there is the outflow of the purchasing cost; at the end, there is the inflow of the scrap sale (sale price for an earlier market exit plan).

Now let's return to our main topic, the data relevant to appraising an investment. You need three major estimations: freight rate (TCE basis); OPEX; and, the most important input of CAPEX, the interest rate. (This assumes you have already defined the leverage of debt and the spread rate/ risk premium over the base interest.) The conventional method is to calculate the long-term average of the existing data and then use it to estimate the long-term average of the future market (some predictions for the first few years, then a long-term average assuming mean-reverting market). If a shipping investor were to ask their chief financial officer for an investment appraisal, they would probably be given this kind of data and assessments in spreadsheets. The critical questions are how much of the existing data should be included in the long-term averaging, and why?

For example, if you want to calculate the long-term average of time charter rates, you may find a time series for decades of the market. Do you use the entire data series? Just the last ten years? Some other subset? The recent data would be useful in terms of deriving the current levels of the market. On the other hand, it may be misleading, since the current market may be an outlier, like the economic boom of 2003–2008. This is a more complex question than most people think.

Once, I attempted to calculate the so-called retrospective data setting with one of my colleagues. This refers to estimating the optimal length of historical data to use in determining a ship's valuation using the discounted cash flow (DCF) method. Our reference for validation was the valuation of known future cash flow. Let's say we have 20 years of data. In middle of the data, at year 10, we can calculate the valuation for both the unknown future (using the historical data of the previous ten years) and the known future (using actual future data). The 'unknown future' refers to the forward-looking case of an expert for valuation at that particular year. We used a variety of data lengths and compared it to the realized values. We found some results for a variety of project samples with the limited capabilities of econometrics.

The results of this study also contribute to our investment appraisal problem. It shows us that we cannot assume a constant length of time for long-term estimations on a variety of projects. Every ship project (type, tonnage, age) has its own specific length of data. We need to be critical about the data estimations and the time assumptions. One can easily manipulate these spreadsheet calculations with some pink adjustments, as I demonstrated earlier. A longer-term data set allows you to eliminate the drawbacks of outliers, while a shorter-term data set allows you to capture the current market levels, knowing that the long-term average of freight rates have historically grown, based on natural inflation.

In this chapter, I have simply presented the drawbacks that inherently come with using data to appraise potential shipping investments. I encourage you to be skeptical of every data source and to improve your analytical capabilities. Every time you read a report, examine the rationale behind what was included and excluded. Best of all, collect and format the data yourself, staying aware of your own self-serving and confirmatory biases.

5 Information asymmetry
What you know and what you do not know!

Short-termism • *Adverse selection*
Professional advice • *Moral hazard*

The neoclassical economic model assumes that actors in the market have all available information and that no one benefits from having some extraordinary intelligence. This assumption is the basis for the efficient market hypothesis. Various economists have proposed the asymmetric information theory that points to possible irregularities or arbitrage opportunities in the market due to a lack of information, which creates particular advantage to a small selected group that gathers such information (see, for example, Stiglitz and Weiss, 1981). The asymmetric information is difficult to detect by outsiders, so you may not even be aware of its existence. However, it is not an overstatement to say that there is always asymmetric information in the shipping business. For example, a good prediction or insider information is asymmetric information. If everybody knew it, it would not be of value; therefore, only a select group of firms or people have the information.

Motives of the directors

A typical shipping company has a number of top managers, including the CEO, CFO, COO, and the rest of the C-suite. A board of directors is full of chief execs, the shipowner, and also some independent directors. There is a special kind of relationship between the chief execs and the shipowner. The shipowner requires good profits to compensate him for the huge capital risk he made. The primary considerations when dealing with the shipowner are how patient he is and what period of financial figures he cares about.

The majority of shipowners are 'short-termers' (whether they accept this or not), and so they usually focus on short-term company figures, such as quarterly profits, while placing less importance on long-term results. Recent market data supports this view. During a peak market, many firms jump on the ship-owning bandwagon. Only a few of these have a long-term perspective and are also able to ride the market crashes. Very few shipping investors try to balance the short term and the long term.

In principle, the chief execs are responsible for the success of the company; in practice, they are responsible for satisfying their boss. They have incentives to achieve what the shipowner wants. When they deliver those things, they secure their position, their competitive salary, etc. But these things are not necessarily in the best interest of the company in the long term.

As such, a shipowner should be on-site and in regular contact with the accountants and the rest of the staff. Lazy shipowners prefer to enjoy their status (again, the 'king of the seas' factor) rather than spending significant time understanding their firm. A savvy shipowner, however, knows everything that happens and never allows his pride of ownership to affect his critical judgment. Some shipowners prefer to outsource everything to a third-party ship management company. They prefer investment managers rather than technical experts. Even this, though, does not completely eliminate the impact of short-term biases.

The difference between the top managers and the shipowner is the asymmetry of information. If the shipowner is more of an observer and advisor rather than operator, an unfavorable outcome can arise. When a manager knows much more than the shipowner himself, it provides the manager a high degree of flexibility and can practice adverse selection. In behavioral economics, the moral hazard is an essential topic. When managers do not care about the morality of the information they share with the shipowner, they can manipulate the business to serve their own interests at the expense of the owner's.

Adverse selection works like this. A shipping company has several options for future investments and has to make a series of critical decisions about the state of its shipping assets. There are a variety of projections and some options to profit in the short term at the expense of long-term prosperity. Ideally, the business should find the balance between the two. However, if all the decisions are left entirely up to the chief execs, the shipowner is inviting problems. Rationally, the chief execs have an incentive to sacrifice long-term sustainability (after they have moved on to other positions or retired) in favor of short-term profits (that may be linked to their bonuses, immediate job security, and so on).

Shipowners should be skeptical about what they know and what they probably don't know, and they should have the company's managers' incentives aligned with the right priorities.

Asset play

We know that asset play is the basis for shipping asset management. However, it is not easy to recognize the cycles and time the market. Everybody wants to know what stage of the business cycle we are currently in and where it is going. Once we have proper answers to these questions, it is not difficult to define strategies. Although it is not easy to pinpoint the state of the market, some experts can show you roughly where it is at. This is an example of asymmetric information and why some companies have exclusive contracts with shipping consultants. Effective asset play requires asymmetric information.

Fear professional advice

There are many different kinds of intermediaries in the shipping industry: shipbrokers, advisors, insurers, port agents, and so on. All of them connect the shipowner to a particular branch of the industry. I will discuss the nature of intermediaries in a later chapter, but here allow me to discuss them in the context of asymmetric information. Since you need an intermediary for a specific transaction, you probably have less information than the intermediaries. Put another way, they know more than you. I once read an interesting critique about such agents that said, "Fear professional advice when it is especially good for the advisor." These are words to live by, as they say. When seeking professional help, it behooves you to question whether the advice is best for you or best for them.

This creates a bit of a paradox: a shipowner needs asymmetric information even as they struggle with asking whether the unknown information is right or not. An advisor typically has several sources of information and selects some pieces to share (a kind of information cocktail). Is there an adverse selection risk here? Probably yes. We arrive at an identical end: moral hazard.

As such, a shipowner must be selective and critical about their advisors. Many advisors, consultant firms, analysts, etc. have strong ties with their customers and particularly care about customer loyalty. This is a sustainable business practice because of the level of integrity with which they provide market knowledge.

Ha-Joon Chang (2014), the eminent professor at the University of Cambridge, emphasized the fact in another way: "Never trust an economist." This very simple argument is among five mnemonic sentences selected by himself in his seminal work *Economics: The User's Guide*.

Seminars, workshops, and courses

As a researcher in the academic arena, I have noticed that there is a basis for information asymmetry based on educational activities. These activities offer you knowledge on a particular topic. If you want to know about a certain topic, it is most likely because you do not know as much about it as you could. You pay for the course and then invest your time in learning. As an added benefit, you have immediate feedback on how competent you are on the topic.

Your instructor presumably knows much more than you, which is why they offer the seminar, lecture, workshop, etc. in the first place. You do not know what exactly will be offered. You just know what the title is. You cannot be sure that all the practical knowledge you need will be provided. If you want to learn about shipping finance, you could find a relevant course with a name that makes you assume you will learn what you need—but you cannot know with certainty until you take the course. A detailed course description may be provided, but it can only give you a degree of confidence.

Ideally, the organizer of the program should have a long résumé, having been vetted by thousands of participants about the quality of their information. They should also demonstrate strong ties with business practitioners. Courses that invite businessmen to share their experience would be very useful and contribute to the quality of the instruction.

Perhaps the most important function of these courses, though, may be networking. In fact, I am sure some programs are created expressly for the purpose of organizing a networking cocktail. Most of the participants know much about the topic already, but they need to reach some key people in the business who cannot be contacted by conventional means. By paying for the course, the participants are paying to interact with these industry leaders.

Then, too, there are other sources of asymmetric information, such as this book. Just the information about the cognitive biases of shipowners may be enough to give you an advantage over your competitors.

6 Emotions
Neuroeconomics of the shipping business

Neuroeconomics ● *Fear and greed*
Amygdala ● *Hormonal factors*
Jump-to-conclusion ● *Blink*

So, first of all, let me assert my firm belief that the only thing we have to fear is...fear itself—nameless, unreasoning, unjustified terror which paralyzes needed efforts to convert retreat into advance.
—Franklin Delano Roosevelt in his inaugural speech of March 4, 1933

You may wonder why you need medical knowledge to be successful in the shipping business. The brain is the least understood mechanism in our bodies. In the last few decades, especially the last few years, we have greatly added to our knowledge base. What we have discovered is fascinating and directly applicable to the economic decisions we make in the shipping industry.

Let's begin with the basics. The human brain can be classified into three main sections. There is the cortex, which is what you usually think of as your brain; the cerebellum, located behind and below the cortex and thought to include more neurons than the cortex. Lastly, there is the limbic system that governs complicated tasks and connects the spinal cord to the rest of the brain. The cortex is further divided into subsections, such as the frontal cortex, credited for judgment and decision-making, as well as other sections that control vision, hearing, language, etc. The cerebellum has a very unique function. It is responsible for all our physical movements, including our balance. Although every section of the brain has its own importance, the limbic system is probably the most relevant to neuroeconomics. Broadly, it manages our emotions and subconscious self. It is also closely related with our endocrine system, which manages hormones and other chemicals that define the rhythm of our bodies and affect our emotional states.

Andrew Lo, a professor at MIT, composed an academic paper reviewing the links between topics in neuroeconomics and our finances (Lo, 2011). He addressed two major drivers of our irrational natures: fear and greed. We know that these two emotions play a part in our decisions, but what Professor Lo presented is the connection between neuroscience and endocrinology. It seems that fear, sex, money matters, risk, gambling, and some other functions of our daily lives are closely related and influenced by the same sections of the limbic system (particularly the amygdala) and similar hormonal steroids.[1]

Dopamine addiction = risk-seeking

Among human hormones, dopamine is the one most related to our economic behavior. When we secrete dopamine, our body physiologically changes (e.g. heart rate, blood pressure, etc.) as it prepares to take on the perceived situation. You may feel it when you are happy, when your fiancé accepts your marriage proposal, or when you gain an unexpected profit. The feeling of being at the top of the freight market is similar. Therefore, we should be cautious about the control of our dopamine drivers. Since dopamine is related to happiness and induces a kind of exhilaration, it rewards our cognitive self by reinforcing certain behaviors. There are two kinds of rewards: material, such as money or recognition; and cognitive—namely, dopamine. For example, intellectual satisfaction is a kind of dopamine reward. When a child is very curious to learn about something, dopamine will be their reward when they make their discovery. Dopamine rewards us when we take on a successful risk, giving us an incentive for the next one.

Of course, you can take this too far. Neuroscientists have coined a term for this: 'dopamine addiction.' If you are repeatedly exposed to dopamine, you may become a dopamine addict. Risk-taking behavior is related with the secretion of dopamine and, thus, is an interesting topic for neuroeconomists. It seems that dopamine levels and risk-taking behaviors are positively correlated. When you are very happy, you tend to take more risks. A kind of self-power (which can easily become overconfidence) is suddenly generated. The more risks you take, the more your body rewards itself with increased levels of dopamine.

Priming effect and neuromarketing

Scientists in this field have also investigated an interesting question: do we have a way to manipulate decisions? (If we had had some dopamine-suppressing drugs during the market boom, it would have been useful!) This is not a question about pharmacology but about external stimuli such as visual cues. For example, monetary symbols and related pictures may promote more selfish behavior and less tolerance. The priming effect is a major instrument for neuromarketing experts. They study primers to find ways to sell more products, like using beautiful models at auto shows. Hopefully, we will find a way to use such primers to help us make better decisions in terms of neuroeconomics.

Rational actors, emotions, and *blink*

Medical research rejects the orthodox doctrine of classical economics. That is, there is no such thing as rational actors (or 'econs'). We are all human beings, replete with emotions and neurologic backgrounds. Our respective levels of dopamine can easily change our perceptions of risk. When they do, we do not care so much about rational decisions. Without emotions, our econometric models would work much better. Then again, maybe not. For example, people with damage to their amygdala are forced to behave completely rationally. They have to recognize and execute every piece of information when making a decision. Their entire life is a burden of thinking and indecisive situations.

Emotions help us simplify problems and the related cognitive process. We use previous experiences to arrive at a snap decision. Our amygdala records our experiences with their corresponding emotional state. Therefore, we remember events influenced by our emotions. When we use these experiences, we also use the emotions behind them. This is Daniel Kahneman's (2011) "fast thinking" or Malcolm Gladwell's (2007) "blink" at work.

In the shipping business, by and large, there is little academic interest in neuroeconomics. The shipping business is a product of human activity: our emotions play a significant role in what happens in the market. The economic bubbles are products of greed, and collapse is driven by fear. We have a great capacity to rationalize our emotions, but we rely far more on our emotions than most people ever suspect.

The role of neuroeconomics is twofold. It helps us to understand our own natures. If you have read some how-to books about the business, you are already informed on issues around decision-making and have probably found some solutions for optimizing the process. Without understanding what you are, though, how can such knowledge help you? Our cognitive self behaves like a less-than-honest advisor: it cannot always be trusted to guide us in the long run. We do need fast thinking and the ability to make snap judgments. However, we should develop our knowledge base about how our minds work and improve our critical judgment about how to deal with this.

***

Why is there a dedicated conclusion for this chapter? At the beginning of the chapter, I assumed you asked why this material was important. If you were patient and read through it, then you are on the right track. But if you skipped it all and jumped to this conclusion for the quick answer, then you are one of the people focused on the short term.

Understanding of emotions is far from useless. In fact, they are essential. Without spending time to understand the basic processes that drive every single decision in the shipping industry, you will be left behind as those with more information pull ahead.

To return to our overarching discussion in this chapter, there is no magical tool to eliminate our cognitive biases. We can only reduce them. That comes from having the right knowledge and then training ourselves to put that knowledge into practice.

When you know what to look out for, you have an early-warning system. When faced with a cognitively difficult decision that sparks fear or euphoria, a note pops up in your mind: "Warning! You're making an emotional decision! Consider your actions!" This can give additional time (even if just a few seconds) to execute decisions with the frontal cortex rather than jumping to decisions driven by the limbic system. Just like training our bodies, training our minds takes time, energy, dedication, and—most of all—patience.

Note

1   For further discussion, see Lo (2017).

7   Alliance capitalism

Solidarity survives

Japanese network economy • Keiretsu
Impatient capital • *Industrial organization*
Long-term competitiveness

When modeling the shipping business, there are a number of options to choose from. For the context of this book, I looked for a business model that minimized irrationality, short-term thinking, and the emotion of impatience yet also examined the incentives for long-term sustainability.

Michael L. Gerlach (1992) coined the phrase "alliance capitalism" to describe the model of Japanese corporate giants. In Japanese, this is called *keiretsu*. The success of alliance capitalism is quite clear. In the Japanese arena, the government plays a big role, but this business system has survived for more than a century. It employs a unique organizational design that allows both long-term growth and competitiveness. The system itself was born in the shipping business and eventually led to what some call 'the Japanese miracle.'

Japan as a product of the shipping business

If you have a look at the history of Japanese business groups, you will come across many shipping firms that have played a significant role in the development of these business groups as well as in the Japanese economic boom. Today these business groups are composed of many subsidiaries, while shipping arms usually have very long histories going back to the 1800s. I will look at some of these business groups and their shipping arms in this chapter. The process of optimizing their shipping business operations took a long time for Japanese business groups, and the history of the industry is, to a degree, the history of Japan.

In the 19th century, there were a few big companies. Two giants still hold such a status even today: the Mitsubishi Group and the Mitsui Group. Before their business operations in electronics, automobiles, food, trains, steel, aircraft, banking, and insurance, they were shipowners. Even today with the vast diversification of these groups, shipping is still a major part of their portfolios.

When speaking about Japan's shipping industry, I should also mention the Kawasaki Group. Before becoming known for motorcycles, manufacturing engines for Boeing, or constructing the Eurotunnel, Kawasaki built and operated ships through its Kawasaki Zosen (shipyard) and Kawasaki Kisen Kaisha (steam shipping company, aka K-Line) divisions.

Their success in the shipping industry has fueled Japanese industrial growth. When the country was still considered a developing economy, the government particularly encouraged and supported shipping firms by providing subsidies and other benefits. Today, these three giants are not 'too *big* to fail,' but too well organized in commercial terms. The Japanese network economy is one of the most popular topics in industrial organization and, according to many researchers, a unique example.

Keiretsu: the network of shareholders

Today, there are five or six major *keiretsu* groups, that include companies from a variety of businesses. In addition to the shipping sections (such as NYK of Mitsubishi, MOL of Mitsui, and the K-Line of Dai-Ichi Kangyo Group) and shipyards, they comprise commercial banks, heavy manufacturing, automotive companies, electronics, TV channels, insurers, trading companies, and more. *Keiretsu* is a kind of private solidarity group; most of these companies hold shares in the others. For instance, a shipping company may also be a shareholder in a steel company as well as a commercial bank.

If any member needs a shipping service, there is a shipping company. If a shipping company needs a loan, there is a commercial bank. If a shipyard needs steel plates, there is a steel foundry that is also the supplier to said shipping company. Most of the contracts are long term. Everything is fixed for 10 to 15 years and, as such, the risk is quite limited.

Based on the Japanese example, I do not mean a shipping company should have other businesses too, but such a long-term collaboration would benefit all parties. When the shipowner and the charterer have mutual interests, it leads to beneficial negotiations and long-term sustainability.

Empathy

In conventional business practices, a shipping company is happy when the market recovers and unhappy when the market collapses. The relative difference between what they expect and what they experience spills over to the shipowners' other cognitive functions. Therefore, they need a countermeasure. If a shipowner also holds ownership in a manufacturer that needs shipping services, the satisfaction of being a charterer will help them maintain their emotional equilibrium. Under these circumstances, there is a reason for also being excited in low freight rates: shipping costs are very low. Being solely a shipowner can lead to faulty reasoning and imbalance of business operations. Long-term collaboration between charterers and shipowners creates a more rational and sustainable basis for remaining clear-headed. Unfortunately, the common practice today is for one side to win at the other's expense. Charterers are king for a while, and then shipowners reclaim the throne.

Solidarity wins; the unilateral approach loses. The Japanese shipping miracle is based on a simple rule: build long-term relationships with charterers at a reasonable and small profit margin. This approach naturally eliminates aggressive marketing and a short-term approach to capital investments. Sustainable growth always survives and thrives.[1]

Last but not least, the emergence of the Ocean Network Express (ONE), a joint venture of three liner shipping firms, is a historical moment for the industry. Three large container shipping arms, NYK, MOL and K-Line, decided to merge their liner shipping operations under a single unique company due to fierce competition and the new structure of the container shipping market. No one would expect such a radical and extraordinary move from any other group of shipping firms. There are so many commercial and financial difficulties in achieving such collaborative work and gaining synergy which these shipping firms have successfully overcome.

Note

1 It is obvious that many Japanese shipping firms suffer from the shrinking domestic market. Today, Japanese shipping firms are expanding their overseas presence and search for overseas business deals much more than at any other time in the history. Since many Japanese manufacturers have shifted their production facilities to other countries, there are some changes in the Japanese shipping industry scene.

8 Cycles

This time, it's almost the same!

Business cycles • Long-term freight index
Centennial decline

Curiously, the economic history of the shipping business is studied more by mainstream economists than maritime economists. It seems maritime economists devote less attention to the history of economic thought and business strategies than their mainstream colleagues.[1] This mirrors the business itself in that most people just talk about the last market boom and the next likely collapse. Many do not consider what lessons can be learned from the past. Our industry has a preoccupation with the present and an overconfidence about the future. We do not feel that we need to look behind us.

The economic history of the shipping business is fascinating and illustrative. The real lessons to be learned are there in the midst of economic ups and downs, crises, warfare, technological shifts, political change, and more. If we want to prosper in the shipping business, we should first know who has prospered in the past and how they did it.

Cycle of cycles

The business cycle model is an essential topic in economics. This theory posits that small cycles are just part of bigger ones. At the edge, we have very large cycles composed of a series of smaller cycles, each with a peak, decline, recession, and recovery period. At the extreme of these long-term cycles, the 200-year industrial cycle model was first proposed by Jay Forrester (1961), the father of system dynamics. Since our existing data is limited, we are still not sure about the nature of the very large cycles. However, we are sure that there is a renewing and iterative system in the economy.

After 2007, some academic publishers began to use industrial document scanning facilities to transfer old hard copies to electronic databases. Many old studies became available to download electronically and review (as opposed to spending days or months in libraries). As a result, researchers had new freight rate data to use for analysis. Previously, we only had data from few sources that went back as far as the end of the 1800s. Now we have far more data, as you can see from Figure 8.1.

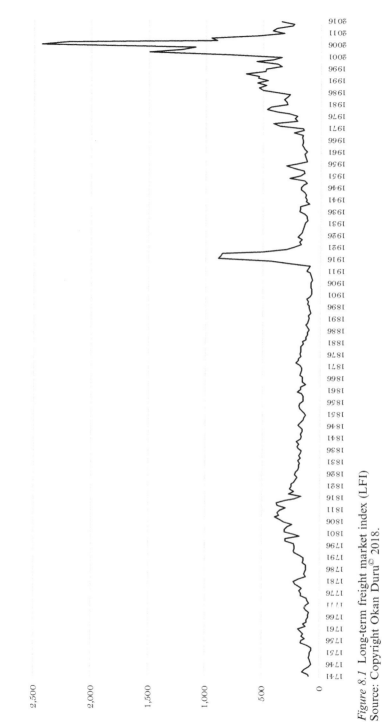

Figure 8.1 Long-term freight market index (LFI)
Source: Copyright Okan Duru© 2018.

In 2009, I collected several freight rate data sources and calculated a long-term continuous freight rate index (LFI).[2] I knew that the data may not be robust due to various technological changes, cargo handling, and pricing techniques, but that illustrating shipping cycles in a single diagram would help to understand trends for the future of shipping. As a disclaimer, I cannot be confident about direct comparison within the data. For instance, we cannot say that an LFI of 500 in the 1800s can directly compare to an LFI of 500 in the 1900s. Even if our conclusions are somewhat shaky, these data can still serve to illustrate the underlying business cycles. In as far as we represent the cyclicality of the shipping market in the particular time frame, it will be feasible to extract some information.

Figure 8.1 tells many stories, but for now let's just focus on the cycles. The centennial decline of the 1800s is a distinct topic in the history of economics and the interest of some Nobel Prize winners. For institutional economists, the 1800s is a unique example of how innovations and institutional changes have created productivity gains and changed the scene of global economics. Another interesting outcome of this diagram is the growing amplitude of cycles in the second half of the 1700s and 1900s. Please zoom in on the data and look at Figure 8.2.

Let me clarify what we are looking at. The 1700s was the period of sailing ships. At that time, we did not have bulk carriers or tankers. Vessels carried bales and barrels together. Also, it was the period of a kind of shipping monopoly led by the British Navigation Acts.[3] Ships spent months at sea for each trip. Now consider the 1900s with supertankers, the Panama Canal, the closure of the Suez, the Iran–Iraq War, etc.

Regardless of the distinct dissimilarities, these two periods show a remarkable correlation in many shipping cycles. Such a coincidence between two distinct centuries raises questions about drivers of business cycles and their lifespans.

Again, we have to be careful about what conclusions we draw from these two disparate data sets. However, at the very least, the work of Reinhart and Rogoff (2009) on the eight centuries of financial crisis, *This Time is Different: Eight Centuries of Financial Folly*, confirms that we should not expect significant change regarding business cycles. As history shows us, the financial markets continually experience ups and downs. Regardless of what ships were built or how we organized the economy, the incentives and emotional weaknesses behind our conscious selves have not changed over time.

***

We learn from history that we learn nothing from history.

George Bernard Shaw

It is easy to criticize, but it is better to ask the question of why we have not collectively learned from history? Why can't we design a sustainable economic environment? Why do we always jump and fall? Whether it is a dopamine

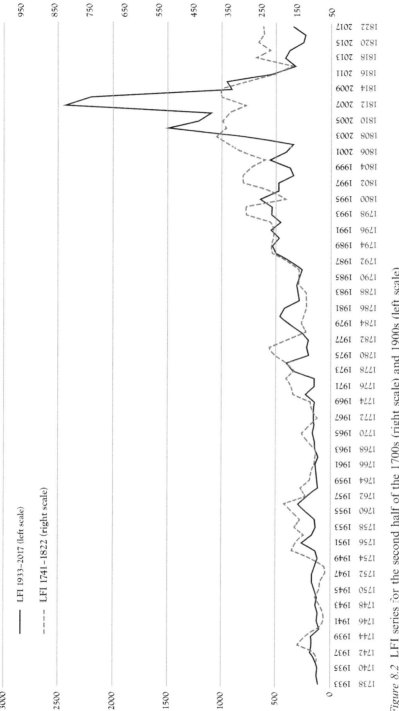

Figure 8.2 LFI series for the second half of the 1700s (right scale) and 1900s (left scale)

addiction, the love of risk, or something else, no one knows exactly. All we know is that we have not learned much from the economic history of the shipping industry. I should particularly mention the efforts of the International Maritime Economic History Association (IMEHA)[4] on developing awareness of and research focus on the economic history of maritime industry.

Notes

1 For example, North (1958), Yasuba (1978), Sager and Fischer (1979), Harley (1989), Craig (2003), Sutcliffe (2016), among others.
2 LFI data is available at www.okanduru.com. Stopford (2009) also presented a similar data set earlier in 2009. It seems Stopford (2009) excluded some data sets that I utilized in the LFI, but both indices roughly represent the ups and downs of the market.
3 It is also a controversy whether the Navigation Acts were, to some extent, among the causes of the American Revolution and the Napoleonic Wars (1803–1815). See Sawers (1992).
4 Information about the IMEHA is available at www.imeha.net.

9 The anatomy of a shipping crisis
Dissection of irrational exuberance

Global trade • Banking system
Bullwhip effect • Asset play • The shipping casino
Freight derivatives • Wisdom of crowds

Professionals in the industry usually point to the global economic climate as the source of shipping market collapses. For example, a financial crisis is often a precursor to a shipping crash. The interaction between global economic activity and shipping services is unavoidable. Since the shipping service is a derived demand created by global trading activities and the overall volume of consumption, any changes in trade and consumption trends will, in turn, produce a supply gap. The supply of shipping—that is, the global shipping fleet—has a static capacity in the short term. Shipbuilding takes a long time, and during peak markets some shipowners cannot even find a free slot in a shipyard. Therefore, the volume of shipping supply does not change quickly. It requires time to balance the supply side of the equation.

The global link

The leading edge of a shipping crisis can be found in the dynamics of the global economy. It is best to look at the role of the financial system first. The major function of the global financial system is to fund projects. However, it is expected that these sources of funds are allocated to projects that add value, that are feasible, and that have real potential rather than toxic projects that do not offer a return on investment.

The primary part of a financial crisis is related to the assessment, selection, and monitoring of proposals. When the system works well, credible and suitable projects can be filtered from the portfolio of proposals. If the filtration process does not work properly, then toxic proposals will find funds. That toxicity can eventually produce what we call a financial crisis. Subprime lending is one recent example of the toxicity problem.

We should add one more dimension to our investigation: the incentives of the lenders. If we ignore the drivers of the banking system, most of the picture will be out of focus. Banking is a profit-making business. Banks provide a link between the capital surplus and the capital deficit. In other words, they collect capital under certain obligations (an interest payback) and resell the capital to borrowers under certain obligations. Some institutions actually apply for cheaper funding from some lenders (e.g. larger banks, pension funds, etc.) and then earn a premium over the cost of capital. In addition to this, the existing fractional reserve banking system also creates money (money creation process) through lending activities. For many, the money creation system is the sole reason for the financial instability of the last century.

Collateral (e.g. mortgages for houses and titles for ships) serves as a safeguard against credit default. In case of a default, banks can proceed to foreclosure and sell those assets in exchange for cash.

The international regulations for risk management in the banking industry (known as the Basel Accords) were expected to reduce risks by increasing the cash cushions (minimum capital reserve) and by establishing some risk assessment standards (e.g. value at risk, or VaR). However, none of these attempts have completely cured the banking system problems. The existing nature of the banking industry (e.g. money creation system, the subjectivity of risk assessments, etc.) is subject to further crises.

Loans

Since banking is a profit-making business, bankers tend to have more customers (i.e. borrowers) when everything is going well or, at least, is expected to go well. There are some additional incentives for relaxing the tight assessment procedures, such as collateralized debt obligations (CDOs) or credit swaps. This relaxation of common sense allows bankers to take more risks. A minimum value covenant helps control the value of ships against the incapacity to service debt. However, it is not so straightforward when the market declines sharply. Nobody wants to buy a ship then. Therefore, the practicality of minimum value monitoring seems to be somewhat overemphasized.

Another concern is how frequently these valuations are performed. If it is semi-annually, we should remember that a ship can lose an enormous part of her value in a six-month period. For example, a 10-year-old Panamax bulk carrier was valued at around US$60 million in 2008, but the value declined to just US$25 million by 2009. Under the mean leverage ratio (70%) and minimum value ratio (e.g. 125%), the value of a Panamax bulk carrier should have been over US$53 million, which roughly meant a US$30 million deficit between the required threshold and the market price. It is clear that minimum value monitoring helps neither bankers nor shipowners.

On the other hand, shipowners still tend to have a high leverage ratio (over 60%) in a peak market. Good asset play can mean prospering in shipping, while bad asset play can wipe out the investment. A bulky shipping portfolio is usually created at the peak of shipping markets. Shipyards are well utilized and even set for several years. The volume of sale and purchase activities increases rapidly, and optimism attracts newcomers into the industry. Most of the newcomers are inexperienced, and their intermediaries tend to draw a bright picture about the business (i.e. about their commission incentive).

Bullwhip effect

In supply-chain management, the term 'bullwhip effect' is frequently used to illustrate the gap between the demand required and the supply provided. A marginal increase in product sales will be recognized by the seller as well as the manufacturer after a period of time. At this point, the manufacturer decides to increase production to supply the marginal increase. Finally, the products will be delivered to the retailer. The entire process of supplying a marginal increase takes a period of time that creates a lag between the demand and its fulfillment. Although manufacturers may respond to the new state of the market, this does not automatically secure the sustainable demand of those sales. Even while the manufacturer is supplying more of the product, the demand may be reduced as a result of external factors (e.g. global trends). Therefore, the marginal volume of the products supplied may be far over the expected demand. The marginal volume of products in the inventory at the time of declining demand will result in a liquidity problem since the inventory cannot be exchanged for cash. This is the bullwhip effect.

The supply of shipping services is subject to the same dynamics as the manufacturing industry. However, the time lag is much longer than the typical manufacturing process. In the worst-case scenario, a new building project can be completed in around two years after the contract is signed. However, it may take more than three years to reach the market peak where the increased capacity is really needed. These situations create a challenging decision for shipowners as to whether to contract shipbuilding during the turbulent periods in markets. Some of them take the risk, while others prefer to remain in their current position. In the shipping market, anything can happen after three full years. However, the positive mood of the industry, triggered by the marvelous price of freight, can paint a rosy picture of the future, resulting in shipyards with full order books.

Drunk with the dreams of asset play

Asset play is one of the most repeated terms in the industry. It also drives shipping crises. There are many misconceptions around this term, and investors sometimes tend to play the wrong game with the wrong rules. Stocks and ships are two different assets. There is opportunity for arbitrage in stock markets; this is not a viable concept in the very tangible world of shipping. Arbitrage efforts are related to asymmetric knowledge as well as the speed with which you capitalize on that knowledge. A stock can be shifted between hands rapidly, while it requires months to do the same with a shipping asset. Asset play can be confused with arbitrage, and this can be detrimental for a shipping investor.

When you look at board games or puzzles, you may find an information section on the box. This section gives you details about the minimum age, the number of players, the average time to play, etc. If asset play were such a game, you would find something like Figure 9.1 on the box.

If a shipping asset is not played according to the rules, you will lose the game. If enough people lose, there will be a market crash. Among these rules, my particular interest is on the overvaluation of assets. The value of a ship is theoretically the present value of all future cash flows in its economic life, such as revenues, costs, demolition, etc. The discounted cash flow method can estimate this value. However, the discounting-based valuation methods work only under regular market conditions. Before the mid-1990s, discounted cash flow, or DCF, calculations could estimate the value accurately. A DCF valuation in 1995 probably discounted the revenues and costs from 1996 to the end of the 2000s. By using the average levels of the previous period (that is, using historical data for a long-term average), a DCF valuation then would be five times less than the DCF calculation performed with actual revenues and costs known today.

For practical purposes, the value of a ship is usually the market price for a potential buyer or seller. One of the drivers of a shipping crisis is the mark-to-market valuation. During times of high expectations, ships are irrationally overpriced. A ship can have a value three or four times greater than she can produce in her economic life. Why do investors tend to pay so much for a ship? The reason is the arbitrage option. Some investors think that they can gain in the short term, for a few months or years, by purchasing the ships cheaply and selling them at a higher price. This results in 'super play' wherein they expect profit margins through a couple of short-term swings. Luckily for such investors, these super plays reaped huge profits between 2004 and 2007.

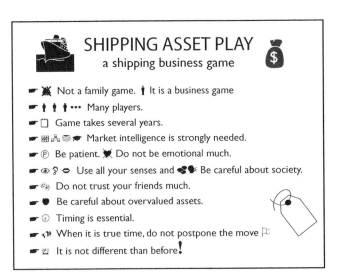

Figure 9.1 Rules of shipping asset play

However, the streak ended and prices came back to grounded reality. The pricing bubble popped, which multiplied the effects of the market downturn.

Let me present a fundamental rule: happiness is the relative gap between reality and the experienced phenomena. Some scholars say, "Happiness equals reality minus experience." In other words, to be happy, expect less. When the market is fruitful, our expectations are very high, which in turn makes us vulnerable to upsets in the market. Therefore, a downward trend has a multiplier effect on society's mood. This can lead to more marked decline than the market would have experienced otherwise.

Shipping casino vs. hedging the risk

Almost by definition, betting is essential for any kind of gambling. You gamble on an outcome (e.g. a hand of cards or a number). If lucky, you win. If you guessed wrong, you lose. However, gambling introduces a whole host of incentives that can affect fair play in certain games. For instances, baseball and soccer players cannot bet on their own matches, nor any match in the league. In fair conditions, the gambler is independent of the mechanism and cannot influence the outcome. In case of derivative markets, we have a similar scheme, though with a slight—but significant—difference. A financial derivative is derived from a physical market, the underlying market defining settlement prices. So, in fact, a trader's approach can make a derivative product completely a gambling instrument (lack of market knowledge and information) or a hedging instrument (traded based on some analytical considerations). As far as the hedging prices of buyers and sellers of a derivative product matches, it is broadly a fair deal. Unfortunately, there is no technical or legal instrument to monitor gamblers and hedgers for eliminating implicit gambling activity. The history of derivative markets includes some disappointing experiences due to insolvency of derivative traders after the financial crisis. After setting up new regulations and procedures on clearing systems, derivative markets are much more secure than they were in 2008. However, the mess created by unskilled and ignorant traders will always deceive ordinary people.

***

The reasons behind the subprime mortgage crisis and the subsequent market crash of 2008–2009 has been extensively discussed. A common explanation revolves around credit default swaps, a kind of derivative product. A derivative is a financial product derived from another financial product, such as a stock index, commodity trading contract, or shipping service contract (aka freight derivatives). In a derivative contract, there are two counterparties (the future buyer in the long position and the future seller in the short position), who are betting on a price or a level of index. A derivative contract is a zero-sum game. There is always a winner and a loser. Derivative markets have become popular in the last few decades, and there was a particularly large increase in the market by the 2000s. According to some estimates, the derivatives market (for both exchange traded and over-the-counter trades) reached over one *quadrillion* U.S. dollars.

How does this apply to the shipping industry? If, for example, as a carrier, I bet on the average freight rate of a future period for a Panamax bulk carrier, I would look for a counterparty (i.e. a charterer) who bets on that period too. It would not matter whether I was really a shipowner or not. The entire derivative contract would be settled at the scheduled date, and one party would receive the difference from the actual market price from the loser, with the market broker collecting a commission. No physical shipping service would occur. The actual market just defines who the winner is.

The derivatives market is a state-of-the-art financial innovation that makes it possible to trade on financial products or indicators without any physical obligation. Although futures exchanges are somewhat regulated, the over-the-counter (OTC) market is an unregulated, hidden, and perhaps even immeasurable marketplace. Therefore, derivatives are thought to be the most toxic and unstable of the financial speculation markets. There are a variety of reasons behind this, but the anonymity of the counterparties and the lack of any regulation are two major factors. There are various efforts to minimize or completely eliminate counterparty default risk, and clearing houses (e.g. Singapore Exchange or NASDAQ) and clearing brokers play a significant role in this process.

In freight derivatives, a person can bet on the positions of shipowners and charterers, and even be a shipowner himself. If one would like to be a shipowner but does not have the capital to invest, the freight derivative market (forward freight agreements, or FFAs; freight options) is a way to make anyone a part shipowner with limited capital.

The freight derivatives market has grown enormously since 2000. There are some futures exchange markets for freight market products as well as the anonymous OTC transactions. The real volume of the market, the identity of the players, and many other dimensions are clearly known. It is difficult to gauge how much the freight derivatives market influences the physical market's volatility and rates and vice versa.

A trader in freight markets will need a sort of prediction to define a bid price for a certain future period (most likely the next two to three months and occasionally a calendar year). An execution broker (i.e. FFA broker) will share the bid and search for a counterpart offering the FFA contract. FFA brokers publish 'forward curves' as an indication of the market for various contract periods. The creation of those forward curves is based on transactions and brokers' assessment for a given period of the potential pricing if transaction would arise. A forward curve is not prediction generated by using any mathematical formulation and algorithm! I think this is one of the common misconceptions about FFAs. An FFA can be classified as the sentimental opinions of traders and brokers, but it is not a prediction. Some traders may employ numerical systems to price their FFA bids, so some FFA transactions may reflect underlying predictive study.

As a derivative product, credit default swaps indirectly influence shipping markets through shipping banks. The risk in financing shipping is shared with third parties, and so shipping banks tend to take more risk and raise more funds for the industry when the shipping markets reach a relatively high level. However, the remaining projects are broadly toxic since the vast majority of secure projects were already funded during the downtimes. In other words, the higher the market, the more the toxicity.

The wisdom of crowds

An essential factor in a shipping crisis is the 'herd mentality' or, in other words, sentiment. In every crisis, there are always different reasons behind a sharp decline, such as world politics or specific shipping factors. However, the herd mentality is always identical. The perception and collective action of the crowds can accelerate a market decline, leading to a market crash. Confidence is regained slowly, which is why freight markets rise slowly. That same confidence disappears quickly, which is why the markets drop sharply. People hesitate to believe the recovery while they rapidly internalize the decline. It is frequently said that losses hurt more than gains.

There is an asymmetric balance between good news and bad news. Why do people tend to stay calm when the market recovers, while they tend to be noisy when it turns back? There should be some leading indicators, like the neuroscience we discussed, but I want to address another factor: earning the respect of others to secure authority. If you tell good news but this turns out to be wrong, there is a higher risk of damaging your reputation than if you are right about bad news. When you tell bad news and then the market turns up, you just say that we survived. People can even feel happy with this kind of swing since the experienced outcome is better than the one expected. How a society approves recoveries or collapses is a fundamental question behind crises. According to the 'wisdom of crowds,' the decisions of the masses are more accurate than those of a single individual—but only insomuch as people who compose the crowd are diverse and independent of one another. Otherwise, you get the 'bandwagon effect' or groupthink. With players in the shipping market being so interrelated, anytime one event happens, it quickly ripples out like a stack of dominoes to all corners of the industry.

Think of it like this: in today's busy world, businesspeople quickly pull out their smartphones when they come to a stoplight. Sometimes they are so preoccupied that they miss the green light completely. They wait for others around them to begin moving before they take their eyes off their phone and pay attention to the road again. If everyone is waiting for everyone else to move, it only takes one leader to go and everyone around him automatically follows. In the shipping business, there are many players so integrated that they do not know when to move. They wait for their cue from the others around them. One single action may result in a mass exodus, one way or the other.

10 The shipping mortgage crisis

How ship valuation methods rationalized toxic shipping portfolios and ship covered bonds[1]

Minimum security value • Subprime mortgage
Value at Risk • Credit rating

The U.S. subprime mortgage crisis (home mortgage crisis) is thought to be a major reason behind the great economic slowdown since 2007. There is a global consensus about causes of the crisis, and both the housing bubble and its financial backing, or the credit bubble, have played a significant role. Therefore, 'credit crunch' is used interchangeably to refer to the same crisis. Since 2008, several studies have investigated the direct causes and drivers (motivators) of the subprime mortgage crisis, and the banking industry is frequently identified as the common component of the failure (a remarkable article was written by Joseph Stiglitz in 2009: "The anatomy of a murder: Who killed America's economy?"). Yuliya Demyanyk and Otto van Hemert's (2009) paper titled "Understanding the subprime mortgage crisis" investigated the background of the crisis and indicated some striking conclusions. The financial quality of loans (e.g. credibility of borrower, credit default risk, liquidity risk, etc.) was eroded in the six consecutive years before the crisis, and more surprisingly, securitizers (i.e. mortgage securitizers who monetize the mortgage loans) were well aware of the declining power of credibility and refunding capacity. Another confounding conclusion of Demyanyk and van Hemert was that the problems behind the financial failure could be identified well before the crisis, but high house prices shaded the monitoring mechanism. The subprime mortgage crisis seems to be a mixture of human error and malfunctioning financial architecture.

As the subprime mortgage crisis sparked financial chaos by 2008, the shipping business and ship mortgages were not immune to the misguided banking industry. On October 5, 2012, a top credit rating institution, Moody's, posted the following announcement:

> Moody's Investors Service has today placed on review for downgrade the Aa1 ratings assigned to the public-sector Pfandbriefe (public-sector covered bonds) and the Baa1 ratings assigned to the ship Pfandbriefe (ship covered bonds) issued by HSH Nordbank AG (HSH or the issuer), which

are governed by the German Pfandbrief Act. On 16 December 2011, both covered bonds were downgraded to Aa1 and Baa1 respectively.

The ratings of HSH's mortgage Pfandbriefe, which are currently on review for downgrade, are not affected by this rating announcement.

In 2008, the volume of the global shipping loan market (transaction volume) reached over US$90 billion. HSH Nordbank was the leading shipping bank with a portfolio worth over US$50 billion (the second was DnB Nor, the leading book runner, with a portfolio worth over US$30 billion). Traditionally, shipping banks operate based on the asset-backed mortgage method (ship mortgage). Therefore, the shipping asset value is a critical indicator for monitoring the credit default risk as well as liquidity ratios. The ship covered bonds mentioned in Moody's announcement are a kind of securitization instrument for transferring risks to third parties to some extent. This kind of bond issuing helps lenders to raise more funds and take more risks. The critical question here is how to measure the value of ships as a backing for these security bonds.

There are a number of reasons behind the anomalies in the shipping loan market, including risk handling and ship valuation, which finally caused the ship mortgage crisis that was hidden behind the aftershocks of the 2008 crisis. On December 2, 2009, an article was published on Business Insider Australia, titled "Banks hide shipping losses with The Hamburg Valuation," which frankly disclosed motivations behind the valuation game:

> As ship values soared, so did apparent collateral values backing shipping loans. Yet as ship values then collapsed, the collateral disappeared. This threatens to put, and has put, many debtors in breach of banks' loan covenants.
>
> How can banks avoid coming to terms with the fact that much of their collateral is worth far less than they represent? Scrap mark to market valuation of ships and replace it with a new mark-to-model-driven valuation methodology. Sound familiar?
>
> (Fernando, 2009)

The mechanism behind the subprime mortgage crisis and the ship mortgage crisis does not differ much, and the fundamental drivers seem mostly the same: the imbalance of value and prices, lax regulation of the banking industry, deteriorating incentives (e.g. common equity constraint, value at risk approach), and short-sighted governance.

Interpretation of causality through nested instruments and drivers is not simple. Rather than benefiting from hindsight, one should dissect the case through each of the components and all the legal/substantial evidence to support arguments. Although it is difficult to uncover the whole picture and recognize each incidence of irregularity, we must look beyond the banking industry and shipping firms and investigate the systemic as well as the psychological nature of financial meltdown since the global subprime mortgage crisis. The ship mortgage crisis is understood to be a *well-hidden banking failure* in the shipping business through some system-produced standards such as ship valuation models.

The mortgage loan system and subprime mortgage meltdown

Before analyzing the ship mortgage crisis, it would be useful to review the traditional mortgage system and the subprime mortgage mechanism in the modern banking industry as a state-of-the-art product of financial engineering. The mortgage loan system basically offers a security instrument, a mortgage, for raising large funds. Mortgages ensure trust between lenders and borrowers against borrower insolvency. Related legal mechanisms are established in almost all free markets, and this allows lenders to possess secured properties such as vessels. The repossession (foreclosure) effort is a coercive power acting as a nudging mechanism in terms of behavioral law and economics (a new perspective in both economics and lawmaking). Once the borrower defaults on the loan or fails to satisfy monitoring instruments (e.g. minimum value covenant), the lender may foreclose the contract and sell the ship to recover the funds raised to purchase it.

Mortgages in the sense of collateral or security were first used in the 1930s by the regulations of Federal Housing Administration of U.S. The legal framework offered 80% or more of the loan-to-value leverage, which provided a unique opportunity for Americans to own their own houses. (The remaining portion of the value is required from the borrower as a contribution to the cost; i.e. the down payment.) In the amortization period, borrowers pay back the loan with an interest premium till the payoff date. Finally, the entire ownership of the house (or ship) is transferred to the borrower on the closing of the contract.

While the traditional mortgage mechanism is widely used in the present banking industry, a financial engineering product—the subprime mortgage—has brought a new tier to the system. The term 'subprime' refers to borrowers with higher default risk (low credit rating), and the prime mortgage is the traditional form of mortgage financing. In the prime mortgage system, banks can convert their risks (credit default risk) to cash through bond issuing mechanisms. Mortgage-backed bonds are sold to investors (e.g. pension funds, insurance firms, mutual funds) who gain from repayments of borrowers indirectly (see Figure 10.1). Lenders still gain profit from these transactions through the difference between the interest gained from borrowers and the paid-for bonds, in addition to miscellaneous fees collected at the time of handling the loan agreements.

In the subprime mortgage mechanism, banks create a way of funding risky borrowers. The mortgages collected from subprime borrowers are repackaged in collateralized debt obligations and sold in slices based on the level of risk (safe, risky, etc.). The problem behind the mechanism is the uncertain valuation of properties (i.e. houses). When a slowdown slightly hits the economy, the risky (subprime) borrowers begin to fail and become insolvent. Banks

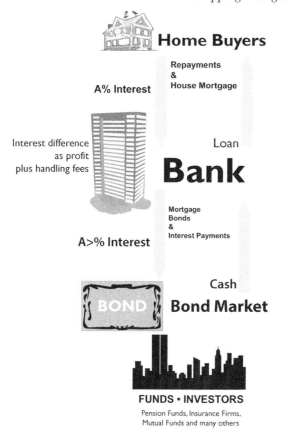

Home Buyers

Repayments
&
A% Interest | House Mortgage

Interest difference | Loan
as profit
plus handling fees | **Bank**

Mortgage
Bonds
&
A>% Interest | Interest Payments

Cash
Bond Market

FUNDS • INVESTORS
Pension Funds, Insurance Firms,
Mutual Funds and many others

Figure 10.1 The system of mortgage-backed bonds
Source: Author.

repossess houses (mortgages) and sell them to recover the outstanding debt. This simple process may well work when a few borrowers default on their credit repayments. However, if the volume of defaults rises enormously, then houses will be nominated for sale as security for the loans. Based on the simple principles of the supply-demand framework, a larger supply of houses will result in lower house prices, and the amount that can be recovered declines extremely. Finally, banks cannot recover the debt properly.

Crisis sparked through the insolvency of borrowers causes a broader panic and loss of confidence, and the subprime mortgage meltdown of 2008 was also ignited when house prices fell dramatically due to panic sales. Therefore, the meaning of security and the risk concerning the value of collaterals has attracted the attention of both financial experts and researchers. The crisis of 2008 is usually thought to be a product of Lehman Brothers' insolvency, but there was actually a more fundamental issue: how to value assets when asset prices oscillate in a massively fluctuating market. The house valuation problem is not an issue just for the banking industry; ship valuation is the second tier of the entire valuation debate.

Liquidity trap and the ship mortgage crisis

The shipping market boom of 2007 (after the previous historical boom of 2004) was the most fruitful and profitable time in the history of maritime industry. The optimism, euphoria, and irrational exuberance of the time are thought to have been driven by repetitive and continuous rise of freight rates (appeal to trend), and these emotional traps triggered fewer critical assessments and less competition neglect on posterior decisions such as ordering new ships or purchasing secondhand assets with asset prices at their highest historically (Duru, 2013, 2014; Greenwood and Hanson, 2013). In a previous study, I investigated the impact of the boom market climate from the perspective of behavioral economics and emphasized the lack of practical implications of shipping market knowledge (information-knowledge vs. action-knowledge). One reason for delayed response or lack of awareness of upcoming oversupply is associated with the rigidity of supply (response of shipyards, production lag, and planning failure delays). The concept of delayed supply response is not new in economics. Cobweb theory illustrates how delayed supply can cause price fluctuations, which are conventionally referred to as business cycles. The underlying principle behind the cobweb theorem is that expectations of economic actors are usually based on looking backwards, and this causes mistaken expectations, ignoring the future state of markets or adjusting slowly (i.e. "competition neglect" in Greenwood and Hanson, 2013).

At the time of the market boom (2004–2007), a massive collective order book had been built up due to the strong demand for shipping services, 'non-storable' shipping spaces. However, there was another factor which encouraged the financing of ships: the availability of 'cheap money.' Lenders were able to have cheaper funds. By the second half of 2007, the U.S. Federal Reserve made a critical decision and decreased interest rates considerably (in contrast to the rest of the world, including the E.U. countries, the U.K., and Japan). This kind of sudden change may happen at times of market crash. The uniqueness of what happened in 2007 comes from the fact that markets were still enjoying prosperity and no other country was decreasing interest rates. The Eurozone even increased interest rates slightly. The impact of this unusual interest rate decline is the liquidity trap. Since Treasury bills and other secure investment options were no longer earning much, large-scale investment banks have turned to industries and/or funding other regional/national banks. Cheaper and lax funding trends also sparked shipping finance. Philippe Louis-Dreyfus described its impact as follows:

> Banks put pressure on the shipowners to accept money almost for free, and sometimes offering 100 percent financing with no equity at all. So, banks have played the very awkward, if not the perverse, role in

proposing cheap money to shipowners who not only didn't deserve it, but didn't really even want it.

(In *Dynasties of the Sea* by Lori Ann LaRocco, 2012)

The traditional method of ship financing relies on collateral security, usually ship mortgages. As with house mortgages, a shipping bank is able to to repossess the financed ship in cases where the borrower defaults. Banks can sell and recover the debt. Since ship prices are quite fluctuant, periodical tests of asset value are needed to check whether the underlying asset has capacity for recovering the debt in case of a default. The mechanism of periodical asset valuation is governed by the minimum value covenant in loan agreements. If the value of a ship declines below the minimum value constraint (e.g. 120% of the remaining debt), then the shipping bank will foreclose the contract and make plans to sell and recover the debt. Without a minimum value test, it may be too late to foreclose, since the asset price may be far below the remaining debt.

Figure 10.2 illustrates the entire mechanism of ship mortgages and ship covered bonds. Shipping banks monitor loan agreements (risk assessment) through minimum value constraint, liquidity ratios, among other things. On the other hand, financial regulators monitor the banking industry through a

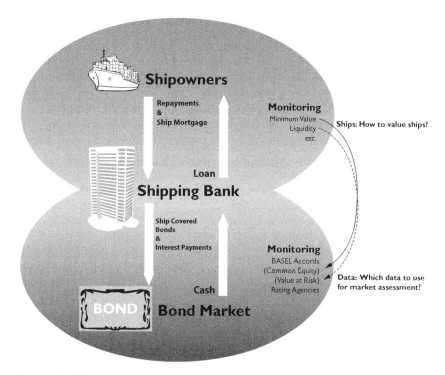

Figure 10.2 Ship mortgage system and ship covered (mortgage-backed) bonds

number of legislative instruments, such as Basel Accords (e.g. Basel III). Basel Accords require some control procedures and risk exposure limits. For example, banks should have a minimum common equity of 7% (Basel III) and should review some risk measures, such as the Value at Risk (VaR) indicator. In addition to the regulators' stance, independent rating agencies (e.g. Moody's) review and rate the credibility of lenders as well as borrowers.

A critical connection to shipping loans and common equity arises from the 'negative equity' debate. When the value of an asset (ship) is less than the remaining loan, then the difference causes negative equity. Therefore, the ship valuation method also contributes to measuring the equity as an indicator for Basel standards.

The VaR approach presents us with some tough questions about monitoring shipping loans. In his mind-blowing book *The Number That Killed Us: A Story of Modern Banking, Flawed Mathematics, and a Big Financial Crisis*, Pablo Triana (2011) criticized the principles behind the VaR method and even blames it for being a leading driver of the financial crisis. Although it seems quite objective and fair, several subjective gaps underlie its complicated functions. Selection of distributions or data sets is subject to the arbitrary preferences of experts. The subjective inputs of risk monitoring are among topics currently debated in the banking industry. In particular, regulators find it difficult to slow down funding of toxic loans when there is a boom market. The downturn that follows makes this easier, though it is usually too late for a proper countermeasure.

In the sudden downturn of 2008, ship prices declined significantly and the minimum value mechanism raised a serious problem. Shipping banks have had huge shipping portfolios, and most of these assets were under default risk in terms of contracts while shipowners were somewhat able to pay back. The 'ship mortgage crisis' has been postponed somewhat due to the uncertain and tricky nature of ship valuations. There are several reasons for ship valuations (insurance, company valuation, court sales, etc.) and several methods of valuation. Mark-to-market valuation is simply the potential price of the ship in the current market with the assumption of potential buyers and sellers. In the case of a peak market, there would be many representative sales with similar technical details; thus, one may find a very accurate value of the ship. In the case of a slowdown, it is not easy to find representative sales, and experts tend to estimate prices based on a pseudo-sale scenario. The mark-to-market method is frequently used for minimum value constraint, although it has introduced a massive default problem. As an alternative, shipping banks have begun to use mark-to-model (valuation based on a model estimation) and discounted cash flow (DCF) methods (also income methods).

As a DCF-based valuation method, the Hamburg Ship Valuation Standard (HSVS)—in other words, long-term asset value (LTAV)—was developed and enacted in German law on May 6, 2008. The HSVS method has been used by German banks to eliminate massive foreclosures based on monitoring asset values. In the subprime mortgage crisis, defaults by subprime (risky) borrowers meant that many houses were transferred to bank ownership as these assets were not sufficient repay the outstanding debts due to declining house prices. Therefore, mortgage-backed bonds have lost their credibility, and credit default swap buyers (a kind of insurance for credit default) have begun to write down the insured values. In the ship mortgage crisis, ship covered bonds (ship mortgaged-backed bonds) played a multiplier role. The HSVS saved the shipping portfolio from massive default which may have ignited a further and deeper credit crunch in the shipping industry (very low ship prices, undesirable foreclosures, etc.). It also indirectly saved ship covered bonds from insolvency.

However, the countermeasures did not secure the credit rating of ship covered bonds. The "Schiffspfandbriefe" (ship covered bond) of HSH Nordbank was first given top rating (Aaa) by Moody's on September 3, 2007. Then Moody's began to review the bonds for possible downgrade, and the first downgrade (to Aaa3) was declared on May 6, 2009. In the following years, Moody's reviewed the Pfandbriefe of several German Landesbanken and their subsidiaries and downgraded the credit ratings many times. The European Central Bank (ECB) listed some German banks, including HSH Nordbank, Commerzbank AG and Norddeutsche Landesbank Girozentrale, for comprehensive assessment in 2013, and in the same year HSH posted a loss of €814 million, the biggest since 2008.

Moody's report on German shipping lenders in December 2013 indicated "significant asset quality challenges" in 2014 (Moody's Investors Service, 2013). The report also questioned the shipping-focused banks and indicated that "Less diversified banks with significant shipping sector concentrations are the most exposed to persistent stress in the sector."

The International Monetary Fund (IMF) reviewed the German banking industry in 2014 and indicated that

> While work on the ECB's Comprehensive Assessment was still ongoing, the authorities were confident German banks were generally well positioned for the exercise. They noted the continuous and significant improvement in banks' capital ratios over the past several years, *but agreed that shipping loans could be a source of further impairments.*
>
> (International Monetary Fund, 2014)

Several investigations have shown that shipping loans are usually toxic and that it is quite difficult to avoid risks given the volatile nature of shipping markets. None of the conventional countermeasures and financial engineering solutions can precisely settle the fundamental problems of ship valuation and risk assessment. Therefore, we need an outlet for this emerging problem.

Note

1 A version of this chapter was previously published online at *The Maritime Executive* magazine.

11 Glaring tycoons
Survivorship bias

News illusion • Lack of fail stories Good positioning

The power of the media is amazing. As we discussed earlier, the presentation of information and our cognitive awareness are key factors in recognizing, framing, and recording data in our brains. Our relationship with the media is like my favorite slogan: 'give and take, supply and demand.' We cannot only blame the media; we must also take responsibility for what we receive and retain.

In the shipping industry, we have a number of newspapers, magazines, and websites to tell us about the market, the industry, transactions, trade activities, and the gossip of the business. I usually prefer to read the 'society' page first. There are many nice group photos there. The people in the pictures are the leading shipping men and their relatives, and they always have big smiles and glasses of wine. I also like to read stories of CEOs, CFOs, and shipowners. People like success stories.

One of the fascinating discoveries of neuroscience concerns how our own neurons mirror what we perceive. This provides us a degree of empathy. For example, when we see somebody deeply injured, we sometimes feel a degree of their pain. When I watch people bungee jumping, I am afraid for them. A similar process works when we watch or read about other people's experiences. This is why success stories sell so well. We want to connect with people that we think are successful, front runners, amazing, or beautiful. Mirror neurons make us feel, to a degree, like we share those attributes. However, this can also mislead us.

Hidden data of failures

Human beings are usually proud of themselves and are often overconfident. We want to see our successes, not our failures. Therefore, our failures are generally ignored and easily forgotten. Thankfully, our memory recording system is governed by the limbic system rather than the emotional center. It is like a key circuit. Our memories are cropped, revised, adjusted, and finally recorded emotionally. I once read an academic paper about the statistics of failed trials. Scientific experiments have failed as well as successful outcomes.

However, academic papers and scientific news rarely report the failed trials. We like to focus on our successes.

For example, the pharmacology industry is huge. Their laboratories conduct thousands of drug experiments to find something that works well on our body. As a result of these experiments, we know only about the successful ones at the drug stores; we know nothing about all the failed trials. Failures are usually hidden and people hesitate to declare them. For example, authors do not declare how many times their books were rejected. We just know about their successes. Without any knowledge of what led to that success, we think of the process as painless and effortless, free from any kind of problem. This is what we call 'survivorship bias': survivors are on the stage; losers run away!

Success is never easy. There is no shortcut for being a successful shipping tycoon. When it comes to those we can learn from, we should heed not only their good experiences and achievements but also their difficulties and failures. If we only demand success stories and do not credit failures, the media will deliver what we want, but not necessarily all that we need.

Luck or good positioning?

Dynasties of the Sea by Lori Ann LaRocco is a fantastic book about the leading people in the shipping industry. The author presents interviews with these individuals as well as notes about her impressions. What I found fascinating, straight from the mouths of our industry's leaders, was the emphasis on behavioral aspects of shipping. They confessed how important a role herding, emotions, patience, and so on play in the business. In addition, there were stories of difficult times, long histories, radical decisions, etc. Also, they pointed out how lucky they were.

We may credit some of their luck to random gifts. On the other hand, we should also consider the importance of good positioning. For all successful people, there is only one common attribute: continuous hard work. Their level of intelligence does not really determine their level of success. They are, of course, smart people, but not the kind of smart we usually think of. They do two things: they work hard and have good positioning. (If I could add one more thing—they enjoy what they do. Their work is their hobby and an enjoyable part of their daily lives.)

What do I mean by good positioning? It is being in the right place at the right time in the market. With a good position, one can capitalize on opportunity; with a bad position, one is constantly reacting to threats. I know some people who are always in a bad position, yet complain about their bad luck. They ignore their own capacity to change their position. In the shipping business, a good position means good deals, strong ties, good communication, good representation, morality, integrity, mutual benefits, give and take, sustainability, and so on.

The outcome of good positioning may seem like luck, but this devalues the decisions made by those leaders before the luck showed up. They are smart people in that they know exactly where to stand—and what to stand on.

12 The fallacy of 'expertise-like' Know-whys

Level of expertise • Shipping consultants
Know-how vs. know-why

A long time ago when I first began my academic career, I was very respectful toward the so-called experts. I read many academic papers and textbooks. I thought an especially thick textbook meant that the author was an especially superior expert. Later, I spent several years reading books, articles, and so on. I developed my first models, drew my own conclusions, and published my own academic papers. After a few more years, I noticed that there was a gap between well-known scientists and the science; that is, a gap between experts and their expertise. By the middle of the 2000s, the academic publishing industry had grown dramatically with many new publishers having been established. Previously, we scientists had to be quite careful about our models and theories since there was a rigorous review process. Today, though, just about any decent research receives invitations from a host of journals and conferences every day.

Do we look for experts with true expertise? Or do we look for 'experts' who can provide some numbers to justify what we want? Did many of today's professionals become experts intentionally or accidentally? From one point of view, an academic paper (e.g. a feasibility report, an investigation) is a scientist's product. Is there perhaps a market for scientists' products? And in every market, are there not substitutes? If you do not like one product, you can buy the alternative. At the very least, we could say that business has influenced the demand for quality expertise.

Shipping consultant

Technical expertise in the business of shipping is vast. When I began my own investigation of its many segments, I could not find where it ended. Even a cursory glance revealed a whole vocabulary and knowledge base that I still have not completely deciphered, despite my years as seafarer, port control authority, private employee, academic, and columnist.

I wonder what an entrepreneur does in this complicated, expertise-laden industry? In fact, a wealth of knowledge may be a real barrier to entry in shipping. If an industry is technically complex and over-regulated, how will a newcomer deal with such enormous problems? The complexity of the technical facet can also lead to deception in the business itself. For instance, if the autopilot of your ship is out of order, you have to pay for an expert in marine electronics to fix it. Do you know how much it should cost? Do you know how long it should take?

To become proficient, you would have to spend a couple years, at minimum, learning the dynamics of the business to eliminate your need for others' expertise. Thankfully, we have many shipping consultants. Actually, every ship brokering and chartering office serves as a type of shipping consultant. In addition, there are those with impressive titles like shipping consultant, shipping advisor, shipping investment consultancy, and so on. Before we get any deeper, though, let me clarify what expertise really means.

Expertise is know-how, but more than that it is '*know-why.*' Everybody uses the term know-how. It is not necessarily difficult to obtain. It can be gleaned from some short courses, graduate courses, seminars, etc. Many experts say they have the know-how. They are absolutely right—no question there. The problem is that they are not really experts since many of them do not have the know-why. What is the know-why? Say that you want to play baseball but you do not know how to play. I can teach you how to throw the ball and how to hit it—the two major tasks of the game. If you can hit and throw balls perfectly, you will be a good baseball player. This is an example of the know-how. What the coach brings to the game is the know-why. Just having the rules and the skills are not enough to manage a baseball team. Plenty of players (like shipowners and shipbrokers) have several years of experience and yet cannot perform as the coach.

How do you find a real expert? That is a good question and also a difficult one. Since there are many tricky aspects, it is difficult to choose the right one from the number of firms and people out there. When you do find an expert, though, you can then proceed to the next step: dealing with a real expert who knows much more than you.

When dealing with an expert

First, do not enter into a job-based contract. Choose either a lump sum payment or a long-term agreement. This is the world of moral hazard. Consider how a plumber or an electrician works: once they come to check out a problem, they always find more than you expected. If you make an annual agreement for services provided, they will be obligated to take care of everything. In the beginning, it may seem expensive to pay for an expert even when there are no problems. However, when a big problem arises, you will be glad that they have a fixed fee. This also incentivizes them to prevent problems before they arise. Thus, you create a true collaborative approach to your business. Get the incentives right!

Second, focus on learning. Begin to study the shipping business, shipping economics, economic history, market trends, leaders' profiles, regulatory environment, and anything else that will inform you about the business. You cannot remain dependent on others' expertise forever.

Third, you need to acquire asymmetric knowledge. Without it, you will remain right where you are with the same knowledge everyone else has access to. If you want to prosper, you need insider information. This might come from consulting with certain established companies, from doing your own research and analyses, or finding niche experts.

Fourth, be aware of the authority bias. You do not have to accept everything provided to you by the experts. They are still human; they make mistakes and experience failures. Do not lose your skepticism and critical judgment at any time, even when everything is going well.

Fifth, be aware of the confirmation bias—especially the fact that it can be used against you. If you debate a point with an expert and they concede the point, you may begin to feel that you are becoming an expert like them. However, if your expert sees that this wins them your approval or more business, then they may begin telling you exactly what you want to hear.

13 Too big to fail
Winner's tragedy

Rationalization • *Overconfidence*
Mobility • *Representation*
Cash abundance

Our brain's ability to rationalize our actions is amazing. It conveniently forgets our failures and allows us to forge ahead. In some ways, this protects us from depression and keeps us from becoming afraid to the point of being paralyzed, although it can also lead to overconfidence. However, the most difficult task may be that of not allowing your friends to help you rationalize your actions and failures. If you become a shipping investor, your volume of friends will increase sharply. There is a strong correlation between becoming a shipowner and the number of 'good' friends you suddenly have. You will be respected and propped up, even when you fail!

The nature of shipowners

In *Dynasties of the Sea* (LaRocco, 2011), some leading shipowners emphasized the role of emotions. All of them pointed to how important it is to control emotions, particularly when everything is going well. In the field of psychology, much of the research on emotion focuses on those who lose something (e.g. a loved one, a relationship, money). There is little focus on winners and the exuberance that comes from winning (e.g. love, a position, material wealth). It is not thought to have much academic value. However, behavioral economics has focused on studying winners in terms of the effects on business sustainability.

A couple of months ago, I performed an informal survey to ask a simple question with simple choices (make your own choice before going forward):

What percent of investors in the shipping business is over the average investor in the industry?
0–15%
16–45%
46–55%
56–85%
86–100%

Even though he is not an economist, Daniel Kahneman is known as the father of behavioral economics and he has won the Nobel Prize in Economics. One of his strengths is that he asks timely questions. The survey question above was adopted from one of Kahneman's questions. The answer to this question is identical for any context and any example, including the shipping business: exactly 50%.

An average investor is in the middle of the population. Therefore, 50% are superior and 50% are inferior. If you estimated over 50%, you are probably optimistic; if less, probably pessimistic. If you are pessimistic about shipping investors, you are probably overconfident about yourself. By definition, most of us are close to average and so experience average success.

Being a shipowner comes with a lot of mental stress. Owning a ship involves more than the basic fact of ownership. Once the shipping investment is made, the shipowner is exposed to the unavoidable optimism of other shipowners. To avoid its impact, you should isolate yourself from the shipping community. These feelings of overconfidence and irrational optimism probably come from a form of natural selection. Who decides to invest in shipping and for what reasons? If you look at the industry, you usually see extraordinary people. They are quite different from investors in, say, textiles, heavy industry, media, electronics, etc.

The three main differences between shipping and more conventional industries are the degree of mobility, the level of representation, and the image. Mobility refers to the fact that most shipping assets are moving 24/7. On the other hand, if I am a textile investor, I can visit my factory, watch my employees, and even have my own dedicated office. In the case of ships, though, investors do not visit their ships often. They see them at the launch ceremony or at the time of purchase, but not much after that.

Like their assets, shipowners become mobile too. A good shipowner is a good representative. A shipowner may be expected to be visible at marine clubs, top conferences, P&I meetings, and elsewhere. To represent your company well, you should have a solid intellectual background, good stature, knowledge about shipping, and so on. You cannot just push your C-level employees to the front and stay behind the scenes yourself.

Finally, there is the image of the shipping business. It is an exotic, cool, and exciting image (all of which contributes to the overconfidence of shipowners). This can be appealing or not, depending on your personality. If you are already a risk-seeking entrepreneur, then you will find this to your liking. But if you have doubts and are risk averse, then shipping will be outside of your comfort zone.

Winner's tragedy

Since overconfidence is the basis for shipping in general, there is a strong chance of experiencing the 'winner's effect.' The typical example of the winner's effect is found in auctions. The winner of the auction is often simultaneously the loser, since an extremely high bid may wipe out the bidder's assets. The major characteristic of the winner's effect is the fuzzy valuation. Firms usually have a maximum bidding value before an auction. However, sometimes they still continue to bid even when the price goes quite a bit higher than their predetermined maximum. The value of an asset is actually twofold: there is the value of the tangibles as well as the intangibles. The more vagueness there is in the tangibles and intangibles, the more irrationality there will be. This vagueness leads to overvaluing the asset.

In the shipping business, the 'winner's tragedy' is also very common, even though we do not name it as such. Here, I do not refer to auctions in shipping, but rather auction-like pricing. For example, do you know how ships were priced in the boom of 2007? At the top of the market, when everything was going well, ships were like money dispensers. Consequently, shipping investors became cash drunk. The more success they experienced, the more overconfident they became. They rationalized that they were 'too big to fail.' However, the more we push our investments to make even more money, the more harmful results we may experience.

Investors ignored the lessons of the past, saying that "this time, it's different!" From our short discussion on the business cycles in shipping, you will have noticed that our motto should really be "this time, it's almost the same." In terms of the ups and downs, there has been no major change in the last three centuries. Carmen M. Reinhart and Kenneth S. Rogoff refer to the last "eight centuries of financial folly" (Reinhart and Rogoff, 2009).

Call it folly, winner's tragedy, or the too-big-to-fail bias—the result is the same.

14 About the C-level executives
Get the incentives right

Chief officers ● *Culture impact*
Perception of Shareholders ● *Groupthink bias*

Alex Ferguson is one of the most memorable personalities in the history of soccer. He managed Manchester United for 28 straight years, an unbelievably amazing feat in the world of professional sports. The directors and managers of soccer teams deal with a number of difficult tasks. They have to win the match, keep the team motivated, keep the fans happy, keep the media frustrated, keep the president proud of the team, and prosper in the long term.

The final objective, however, is usually ignored. Fans look at the present. If their team is not the champion this season, it does not matter whether they prosper in the long term. We have strong short-term memories but a limited perception of the future. Life is short, and we want everything now.

In discussing the Japanese miracle, I spoke about the long-term orientation of firms but did not mention the nature of the top managers. Human resource management in Japan is based mostly on loyalty and age. A top manager is usually over 50 years old, has held several positions, and has supervised many projects. He has been groomed to be a leader for many, many years. Therefore, a top manager has long-term incentives. He knows that even after he leaves his current position, he will still experience the aftereffects of his decisions. Therefore, the sustainable growth of the company is also in his own best personal interests.

Risk-seekers enjoy the noise and oscillations of the market. They think that during those oscillations they can win against the losers. After all, if there is high volatility in the market, it means there are some winners as well as losers. We should make a critical decision about the nature of markets. If we continue to support volatility, we will all be at risk of being among the losers, as no one is too big to fail. Sustainability can result in mutual success if everybody agrees to it. Therefore, prospering in the shipping business is not just the problem of the individual; it is also the problem of society.

Our language, our incentives

Keith Chen is a professor at the University of California who studies behavioral economics. He published an impressive study about the impact of languages on our actions (Chen, 2013). He performed a review of several languages, looking particularly at future tenses. According to his research, cultures that use future tenses tend to have an image of a future far away from them. The future is very fuzzy and they feel more compelled to do something today rather than to plan for tomorrow. When it comes to finance, they tend to see profits in the short term and they spend more than they save. On the other hand, some societies do not use future tenses, such as in Japan, or have a limited sense of it, such as in Germany and Norway. As a result, they save more than other cultures and have more of a long-term orientation.

Thus, we have short-term-oriented cultures and long-term-oriented cultures. This does not mean that everyone who speaks the same language is similarly oriented, but it does have some influence on their natural perspective. If your native language uses more of the future tense, then you may have to compensate for that in your company culture and own personal outlook.

The CEO as a shareholder

It is a common practice to reward top managers with shares of the company based on their longevity and success. I do not know why this is popular in the shipping business, but it should not be. The results of being a shareholder differ according to the type of entity the company is; for example, public companies with IPOs (initial public offerings) vs. private entities such as a limited partnership. Stockholders have short-term incentives, and this influences managerial processes. If the CEO is also a shareholder, the result may be an even greater emphasis on short-term gains at the expense of long-term sustainability.

The problem seems to be related to our monitoring techniques. A shipping investor needs some indicators for monitoring the success of his top managers. Short-term indicators push them to be oriented to the short term, while long-term indicators push them to be more oriented to the long term. However, the way the shipowner measures their performance is what they will focus on. Therefore, shipowners should be careful about the criteria they apply to analyzing their managers' efforts. Most of all, shipowners need patience. In the shipping business, the long term refers to, at minimum, a market cycle of roughly eight to ten years.

I should note one more thing about the board of directors. When people make group decisions, they tend to take on more risks. Since the responsibility is shared, people feel the effects of the risks less keenly. This is called the 'groupthink bias.' Meetings, discussions, and sharing of opinions are good habits. Like everything else, though, too much of a good thing is not good. There is a strong need for professional risk monitoring in today's economy, and many companies already have such departments.

For C-level execs, incentives define their motivation. Monetary incentives may lead to selfishness and impatience. Just being the leader of a shipping company, however, is priceless. You may not necessarily need rewards—you may just need encouragement and empowerment.

15 Spot vs. period
Risk vs. loyalty

Risk-seeking • *Dopamine reward system*
Shipping portfolio • *Recency bias*

There are two major groups of shipping investors: risk-takers and risk-averse owners. Both have their own incentives, advantages, and disadvantages. Our cognitive self naturally likes simplifications and reductions. Therefore, we tend to gravitate toward black-and-white classifications while ignoring the murky areas between the two extremes. Here, I refer to two groups to simplify the explanation, but in real life we definitely have a spectrum between two extremes: somewhat risky; somewhat security-minded; those who want to improve both opportunity and employment risks. To discover the best mix, let's consider two perspectives: that of the 'risk lover' and that of the 'risk reducer.'

The risk lover

You may have heard of the financial twins of risk and return. The relationship between them is one of the most popular topics in finance research. The more risk you take, the more return you may enjoy … *if* everything goes well, *if* you are lucky, or *if* you have asymmetric knowledge. The rationale behind taking or seeking risk (e.g. venture capital, hedge funds) is the potential for enormous profits. Therefore, risk lovers love risk! Risk lovers need the dynamics of a management team for following the market closely, capturing any opportunity, and rapidly defining entry-exit decisions.

For risk lovers, fast thinking is a necessary skill. The problem is that fast thinking can be misleading. Plus, it is naturally exposed to cognitive illusions. As such, fast thinking may not be the necessary skill but, rather, fast *and* critical thinking. The prefrontal cortex manages critical thinking, while the limbic system facilitates fast thinking. When the limbic system takes control, the role of critical thinking is minimized. It has a strong connection to our memories and experiences, giving us the signal to continue on: "You have the experience, you know this business, and you can do it—full steam ahead!" When we do take the risk, the reward is immediate: the sweet rush of dopamine. While this truth is unpleasant, knowledge is better than ignorance.

Risk lovers are a mobile and flexible group of shipping investors. They are experts in speed, multitasking, and representing (i.e. showboating). Risk lovers can easily shift from one position to another and can quickly see the benefits in opportunities. If there is a very cheap bulk carrier, they go for the transaction and then sell it at the peak of the market. However, there is a gut-wrenching gap between what they would like to do and what they are able to do. When they look back on missed opportunities or risks they could have taken, they often feel overwhelmed.

In theory, risk lovers are able to perform fascinating business deals and raise large amounts of capital. In practice, it is not as straightforward as it sounds. There are two typical barriers: our cognitive selves and that of others. When the market begins to decline, everybody wants to sell ships. But when everyone is selling, then who are the buyers? By the time they want to sell, the seller is already late. However, it is difficult to time these transactions ahead of the market decline.

Spot trading matches the needs of risk lovers. If the ship is fixed for the short term, this gives the investor the implicit option at the end of each trip to keep it or sell it. Spot trading is driven by the recent state of global trade and economics. There are some very high peaks and some very low valleys. If you are patient and strong-willed and can exit at the top of the market, you will gain a lot. Otherwise, you will be the loser in the risk-taking game.

Let me remind you of the conclusion of my previously presented research: fear, sex, risk-taking, and gambling are correlated with our endocrinology. We know that the dopamine high is a common reason for risk-taking as it is addictive like cocaine. Patience and a strong will are what you need in order to take control of your economic decisions in the face of such physiological forces.

The risk reducer

For sustainable and painless growth, risks should be eliminated as much as possible. However, the reduction of risk causes a reduction in the rate of return (at least in the short term). This has both direct and indirect benefits. Once you fix your ship for a long-term contract, you do not need to pay the transaction costs for each trip (e.g. the brokerage commissions). Also, you know a good deal about the future of your operations, which gives you the opportunity to improve your costs, business reputation, etc.

In the spot market, you have many customers with a variety of needs. Each contract has a distinct risk exposure. In the period market (time charters), you have just one customer whom you can study. Once you know your customer's needs, you can configure everything based on that. You will be just the carrier and so do not need other procedures, paperwork, and responsibilities. All the voyage-related issues are transferred to the charterer.

Therefore, risk reducers tend to stay in the period market and do the same things every day. It is more than a little unexciting. However, the dopamine reward system works for risk reducers too. The difference is that it is a sustainable reward system. They will not enjoy the historically big bonuses, but neither will they suffer the historically big penalties. They just receive a small yet continuous bonus. The small but repetitive dopamine drip keeps them mildly motivated, but without the euphoria, excitement, panic, and depression.

This sounds good, but risk reducers also have headaches. The reduction of risk requires strong ties with charterers and a strong ability to see things from their point of view. Customer care is a more serious task for reducing risks. To effectively manage this, you may even need a new C-level exec: the chief customer officer. Customer loyalty must be built and secured in order to have the opportunity for long-term contracts (say, over five years). That means having a good ship operation team and particularly good seafarers.

There is also one more thing you need: a young fleet. A charterer does not want to fix an old ship for a long time. They need painless, smooth cargo handling and transportation. Therefore, the quality of the ship and its seafarers play a critical role for risk reducers.

Risk reducers forgo many opportunities because they are stuck in other contracts or long-term agreements. As such, they are generally immobile and inflexible.

Empathy: compromising

Risk reducers are akin to big calculators: they can do a lot of complicated work, but they are a pain to lug around. Risk lovers are like calculators on smartphones: they go everywhere and change functions quickly, but they do not have the range of operations that other calculators do. The trade-off between the two is quite tough. But what if there were a third option like a tablet that balanced mobility with performance?

To discuss the shipping equivalent of this compromise, let's return to my discussion on portfolios. Since a portfolio is a bundle of assets, we may design a bundle of short- and long-term fixed ships. The key question is how to define the mix. What percentage should be allocated in each position? In *Shipping Strategy*, Peter Lorange (2009), one of the great shipping minds, provides some tips. We have two fundamental tasks: asset play and trading. In other words, the shipowner should investigate the investment timing (entry-exit, buy-sell) while trading ships in the short (spot) or long positions (see Figure 15.1). The rules are simple but managing the transitions is difficult.

One more task remains: positioning ourselves in the market. If we know the position of the market, the remaining tasks are relatively easy. We do not know the exact time of its recovery or its decline. We may know that the market is high or low, but we do not know when the turning points will be. Many people and much money have been spent trying to find a way to predict these inflection points. The result is garbage. Since we cannot predict the market, as a compromise, risk reduction should be our basic function. We should pursue risk reduction as the basis of our portfolio and then find other ways of taking risk for higher return.

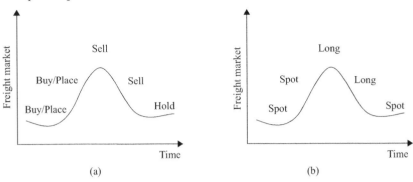

Figure 15.1 The asset management policy (a) and trading policy (b)
Source: Lorange (2009).

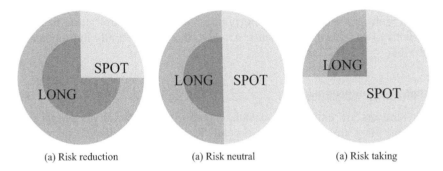

(a) Risk reduction   (a) Risk neutral   (a) Risk taking

Figure 15.2 Shipping portfolio based on the volume of spot-long positions

In a peak market, the shipping investor should define the asset play posi-tion for their existing fleet. Some of the fleet will be taken out of the bundle, and the remaining vessels should be transferred to long positions. To reduce risk, before the collapse of the market, a portfolio should have more long-term contracts and less spot contracts (Figure 15.2a). Once the market col-lapses, the state of the portfolio should be kept as it is for a couple of years. After the initial period of recession (i.e. after two to three years of being in a valley), the portfolio should be adjusted to a fifty–fifty setting before the next recovery (Figure 15.2b). This prepares the portfolio for the next move and ensures risk neutrality. This also pushes the 'buy' button saying it is time to invest in shipping assets because new ships are needed for very long contracts. Secondhand ships and the shipowner's existing fleet are for spot contracts.

Here I need to address the difference between long and very long positions. A long-term contract refers to 1 to 3 years of a fixed position, while a very long position refers to 5 to 15 years of a fixed position. It is probably better to keep one-fourth of a portfolio in very long positions and another one-fourth in the spot position. The remaining half of the portfolio is the dynamic section that can cover long or spot positions accordingly (Figure 15.3).

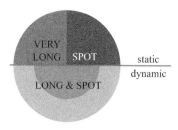

Figure 15.3 Static and dynamic sections of shipping portfolio

When market recovery begins, it is time for the move from being risk-neutral to being risk-taking (Figure 15.2c). It is not difficult to recognize whether the recovery has begun. There are two common signals: a massive premium in freight rates (approximately 100–150% upturn) and the noise of the crowds. Based on the asset play setting of a risk-neutral position, the portfolio gradually converts to a risk-taking position. Since the order book volume is not very high in a recessionary market, the orders of the risk-neutral position can probably be delivered in a couple of years. This is a kind of securitization of the portfolio. After a few years (two to three) at market peak, the portfolio needs to reduce risks and return to long contracts (particularly contracts over four to five years).

The transition between risk-taking and risk reduction pushes the 'sell' button. Now it is harvest time. When the ship-to-cash transformation is complete (except for ships fixed for the very long term), the shipping investor has a strong balance sheet and liquidity.

Don't wait for the turning point

Many shipping investors know firsthand how difficult it is to apply these ideas. We have the status quo/inertia bias working against us, plus the endowment effect and recency bias. They are all supported by overconfidence, the natural optimism of the shipping industry, as well as the strange optimism of lending bankers.

Although bankers know the cyclic behavior well, they tend to loan during peak markets and reduce their loans in declining markets. They make it easy for shipowners to purchase more ships when they are the most expensive and make it difficult to buy the same ships after the market crashes (when shipowners can save 30–50% of the ship's initial value).

Interest rates and the freight market move together. Therefore, a bank loan during a peak market is probably very expensive—this is, of course, what the banker wants to sell. Today, shipping banks and banks with specialized shipping departments are very sophisticated. They know how to take money back. They have many instruments at their disposal, such as collateral, monitoring constraints, covenants, and more. If a shipping investor has a strong balance sheet and high liquidity, this is good news to their bankers, who will do their job and push him to borrow more.

The status quo bias refers to inertia or resistance to change while everything seems to be going well. This is really a form of laziness. I have already mentioned the endowment effect: when we hold a ship, we overvalue its true worth through irrational sentiment. Finally, the recency bias is our tendency to focus on recent data and developments while ignoring the long-term perspective.

Based on the lessons learned in this chapter, a shipping investor needs three fundamental things: capital, knowledge, and a cool head.

16 Too small to survive
Uniqueness vs. size

Economy of scale • Economy of scope
Scope-in, scale-out • Cost leadership

If you are over 40 years old and grew up in a city, you probably remember the small delis and markets on the street corners. Many of these still exist in Manhattan. Elsewhere, though, supermarkets have killed them off. The smaller your business, the less power and flexibility you have. In the crowded streets of New York, there are enough customers that these small shops can still make money. There are enough people that they can specialize in catering to a subgroup's unique demands.

Here we see uniqueness vs. size. However, there are also some street vendors. They are in an even tougher situation (as you can guess from the quality of the food some of them serve). From time to time, business may be relatively good—say, if the Knicks are playing a home game. But this is more often the exception than the rule. The takeaway here is that size matters; and in the shipping business, it matters quite a bit.

Scope and scale

Modernism, postmodernism, and Fordism are academic terms. Instead of investigating the philosophy behind them, let's focus on how they have influenced business and economics in the last half century.

Consider the tailor and his competitor, the textile factory. The tailor measures you, designs your suit, and sews it for you. It is, as they say, tailor-made for your body. A textile factory owner, however, thinks bigger. He has textile machinery, several employees, and capacity for mass production. However, a factory owner has no time to measure each customer and customize their clothing. Instead, the factory has standard sizes that cover the common sizes of the general populace. When you buy a factory-made suit, it somewhat fits you, even though it may be a little long or a little snug. But it's cheaper than paying a tailor and it does the job. The tailor is in the business of scope, while the factory owner is in the business of scale.

In the shipping business, these relate to the two major strategies: pursuing an economy of scale vs. one of scope. Before the 1900s, most industries resembled the approach of the tailor. After that, with the diesel revolution and other developments, the scale economy took over. In the last few decades, though, the needs of mankind have become more specialized and complex. This has resulted in the development of special services that we call the 'scope economy.'

The scale economy focuses on volume and the reduction of costs by creating large volumes of products. The scope economy focuses on the particular needs of customers. For example, in the shipping industry a chemical tanker is a typical example of the scope economy. In the beginning, container transportation was a scope-oriented business. Today, there is also a container market in the scale economy (even while the containers themselves remain a scope business). Therefore, the size of container ships has grown rapidly in the last ten years.

There are two outcomes from the scale-scope trade-off. First, the scale economy is correlated with the market share of a company. Since a scale strategy requires a massive shipping fleet, scale-oriented shipping makes up a big portion of the shipping pie. If you want to be successful in the scale business and have a high return on investment, you have to be of a sufficient size to compete. On the other hand, scope-focused shipowners have a relatively small market share in the shipping business. The level of specialization defines the uniqueness, and more unique shipping creates higher returns (Figure 16.1).

Great portfolio

In discussing shipping portfolios, we did not mention the types of ships that comprise them. There are a few shipping companies with portfolios that consist of several different types of ship (e.g. NYK, Maersk, MOL). For example, a shipping portfolio might consist of a dry bulk fleet, a wet bulk fleet, a container ship fleet, LNG carriers, and product carriers. Taking it down yet another level, the portfolio might be divided even further; for instance, the product tanker fleet might be split into MR, LR1, and LR2 pools.

You may notice that a large shipping portfolio has to consider the mix of its scale and scope fleets. Actually, we can divide a fleet into three groups: scope assets, scale assets, and assets in between (or, as I term it, 'scope-in, scale-out').

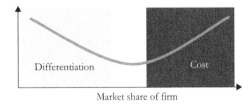

Figure 16.1 Porter's (1980) classification of strategic management

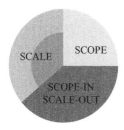

Figure 16.2 Shipping portfolio based on the volume of scope-scale positions

In the container shipping business, we have an interconnected business design including logistics services and liner shipping services. In the logistics division, we have specialized services for transferring cargoes into their containers. There are a variety of containers for common packages, frozen products, pressurized gas products, and even chemicals. This is an example of the scope-in container market.

Varieties of containers are carried to container ports to be loaded onto container ships for liner shipping services. Because of the large volume of containers loaded, this is an example of the scale-out phase. Between shippers and ports, the scope business rules are in progress. When it leaves a port, the scale business begins. Therefore, 'scope-in, scale-out.'

What is your optimal size?

Tailor-made business designs are needed for managing the scope-scale trade-off. We must first measure your business intentions and then find which business strategy fits you. For small players (say, about ten ships), it is better to be in the scope business since it does not require a large fleet. In the scope business, there are many options, such as chemical carriers, product carriers, small LNG-LPG carriers, and other special-purpose ships. They have relatively higher returns in the long term, although the employees need more specific skill sets for handling specialized vehicles and cargoes.

Once over the ten-ship threshold, you can design your business to focus on scale. It does not make sense to be a dry or wet bulk carrier if you only have a few ships. This is like being a street peddler: one bad day (i.e. a market crash) or an accident (i.e. an on-board malfunction) can wipe out your entire business.

17 Seafarers and outsourcing

Bundle it!

Economy of network • Bundling services
Third-party ship management • Crew management

What is the biggest headache in the shipping business? You might guess it was the swings of a highly volatile market. This is indeed one of the biggest problems. However, investors who both own and manage ships have another frustration besides the market for freight: the market for labor. You can understand the size of the problem from the number of employment agencies, particularly in South Asian countries. Although a seafarer can apply to shipping companies individually, there are a host of issues that must be addressed. In this gap sits the employment brokers.

Life at sea is particularly difficult. Just finding someone willing to accept the assignment is one challenge. They have to be away from their families and effectively be cut off from the rest of the world for long periods of time. They are constantly assaulted by the sun and sea. Just having dinner in the middle of choppy waters can be an adventure—and keeping it down can be another.

Then, too, a seafarer must be knowledgeable about the ship, its operations, and their own particular job. They must also be able to communicate all of that knowledge when a port authority agent or safety inspector comes on board. Besides individual traits, a shipping employer must also consider how the employee interacts as part of the crew. Some individuals may excel at their own tasks but be particularly difficult to work with. Then there are also the issues of mixing nationalities and ethnicities. On top of all this, there are also a number of employment regulations that companies must adhere to when hiring someone to man their vessels.

For all of these reasons, most shipping companies find it easier to outsource the assessment and hiring tasks to an agency that specializes in such, leaving the owners and managers to deal with asset play, trading policies, questions of scope vs. scale, and the swells of the market.

Third-party management

The history of outsourcing does not go back very far and is still not a common practice in our industry. However, this is a particularly appealing option for newcomers as it gives them time to master specific issues without having to learn everything all at once. Some third-party providers have aggregated services to act on behalf of their clients. Effectively, they have created a shipping bloc with enormous negotiating power.

Such an organization is known as third-party ship management (TPSM), one of the smartest solutions in the industry. TPSMs are the hot topic nowadays and has taken a position at the forefront of the shipping industry. These organizations have developed key performance indicators for their clients, stay abreast of the latest developments, present at international conferences, arrange financing, and so much more. Operationally, they offer crew management, operations management, commercial management, and just about every other task shipping owners have to take care of. Because of their clout, TPSMs often enjoy preferential rates, discounts, and access generally denied to all but the largest fleet owners.

From an economic viewpoint, TPSMs are ideal for smaller companies who have limited negotiating power. (However, they are so beneficial that plenty of large companies employ their services too.) A TPSM typically charges a management fee, depending on how many vessels you have and the extent of the services required. Many in our industry criticize TPSMs' fees, but they forget just how much it costs to manage these same tasks in-house, with the need for roomy offices, a small army of qualified managers, high salaries, conference rooms, and acres of filing cabinets to deal with all the paperwork of an overregulated industry. Managing your operations in-house is a point of pride for many shipowners, but that goes back to my 'king of the seas' discussion. If a company is big enough that it can enjoy economies of scale by doing it in-house, it still needs to factor in other variables before making a decision, such as the benefits that come from a vast business network and a bigger pool of people who have the know-how and, more importantly, the know-why. These hard-to-measure intangible benefits must be part of any cost–benefit analysis.

Many shipping investors view shipping as a tangible asset-based business. This is a great misconception. The intangibles are more important. If you have strong business ties and a powerful network, you will know that their value is priceless. This is what really made shipping giants and shipping tycoons—not their ships, but their relationships.

18 Dashboard
Visualizing shipping metrics

Automated business management ● *KPIs*
Graphical representation ● *Visual recognition*

We have already discussed the human brain in detail, such as the role of the amygdala and its impact on emotions and memory. Now we turn our attention to the hypothalamus. In addition to its other functions, the hypothalamus works with the autonomic nervous system (ANS) to control our inner body functions without our conscious awareness. Our body has a number of chemical and mechanical rules, and the hypothalamus checks whether the different systems are working as they should. If any indicator sounds an alert, the hypothalamus responds appropriately, such as secreting steroid-like hormones. I want to underline two important characteristics of the ANS: its unconscious nature and its rule-based, autonomous management. The management of an entire human body is not easy. Since the ANS deals with several issues without our awareness, our conscious brain is not subjected to mental overload. Managing all those systems underneath our consciousness requires a set of standards. Therefore, our bodies have rule-based mechanisms with reference levels, limits, boundaries, and benchmarks all embedded in the ANS. Based on these rules, the ANS can increase heart rate, secrete certain chemicals, etc.

In the modern structure of corporate governance, we need an autonomous system like the ANS for the monitoring and control of routine problems without wasting the focus of upper-level executives. Similar to the human body, there are many issues that arise in daily operations, but often the solution to these issues is straightforward. However, every single problem requires a certain allocation of time and effort by managers, resulting in losing focus or outright ignoring other issues. One of the most challenging problems for modern managers is the mental task load. Busy managers do not have time for long-term thinking, creative thinking, and other such important activities. Without ANS-like subroutines, how can upper-level managers ever effectively address long-term issues?

The shipping business has more dimensions and technical complexity than many other industries. It is not surprising that short-term thinking and the corresponding asset management failures are common in shipping. Company managers are required to do an almost overwhelming job, performing conventional management duties as well as struggling with the complexity of the industry, including safety regulations, seafaring, legal disputes, chartering relationships, and moral hazards, among others. You almost have to be Superman to deal with it all.

Snapshot

Monitoring and control are the major duties of top managers. However, these are based on a number of underlying theories and perspectives. Without a comprehensive definition of objectives, perspectives, and horizon, monitoring and control can be an illusory function with no practical value. For example, many shipping companies express that they are long-term focused, while their focus really seems to be on the short term. Many of them have so-called monitoring and control systems, but these serve only the short-term issues.

It is very common to define some initial objectives and later relax them due to 'periodical revision.' Revising an objective is often necessary, but such revisions should be based on rational, credible, and transparent reasons. When the monitoring and control system of a shipping company is based on predefined, robust objectives and perspectives with corresponding rules, it simplifies the task load of managers. This, in turn, allows upper-level executives to focus on more sophisticated and critical problems. But if managers do not have time for self-evaluation in the first place, who will improve the processes?

One of the most useful instruments of monitoring and control systems is the dashboard. It provides an instant picture of the entire company's activities, achievements, gains/losses, and failures. The indicator panel of an automobile is a familiar example of a dashboard. Drivers can find all they need on these panels for maintaining operation of their car. Top managers and shipowners are the drivers of the company and, as such, need an indicator panel just like that in an automobile. There is a stream of academic and commercial interest in designing effective corporate governance dashboards. Every company needs a customized dashboard for its own needs and objectives. A dashboard visualizes useful information that is generated by using data provided from different sections of the company. For example, a dashboard can illustrate the liquidity and long-term indicators for asset management as well as presenting a snapshot of operational activities (e.g. delays, excessive use of funds, etc.).

Data and information visualization have become popular topics in the last decade, with intelligent design of graphical representations (e.g. infographics) being a growing field. The human brain's pattern recognition systems are very effective with well-designed visual objects. Therefore, it is not only a technical matter to design a dashboard but also one of art in order to facilitate pattern recognition and human-computer interaction.

A dashboard has three main components: an interface (visual item output), an execution unit (data manager), and a data collector (data network input).

The interface refers to the visualization or graphical representation unit. There are many ways to represent data, but only a few are useful for effectively managing the indicators. The execution unit is the core item. Based on predefined objectives, perspectives, and rules, the execution unit compiles the input data and generates information for management's consumption. Finally, with the data collector, every division or department of the company enters the corresponding input data into the system. Traditionally, different company sections would prepare weekly reports to submit to management. This meant that the top managers had several related reports but would need to go through the effort of mining the underlying information from them all. Usually an executive assistant would deal with this critical task and prepare a short aggregated report. However, increased bureaucracy and paperwork deteriorated effectiveness and dynamism. In today's world, computer-aided management instruments are essential for even mid-sized organizations.

Priority and scope

There are four primary management priorities of a shipping company under top management (i.e. strategic asset management) level: financial management, fleet management, human resources management, and legal management (see Table 18.1). On one hand, financial management and fleet management are the fundamental departments of a shipping company. On the other hand, human resources management is usually a department of large companies since they have significant office personnel. Moreover, legal management is usually outsourced to independent maritime lawyers.

Table 18.1 A generic organization of a shipping company

1. Strategic Asset Management
2. Financial Management
3. Accounting
4. Liquidity Management
5. Debt Raising and Management
6. Fleet Management
7. Commercial Management
8. Chartering
9. Marketing
10. Technical Management
11. Ship Operation (voyage and port procedures, ship supply etc.)
12. Superintendence
13. Seafaring (in connection with the HRM if it exists)
14. Human Resources Management (HRM) (non-onboard employees)
15. Legal Management

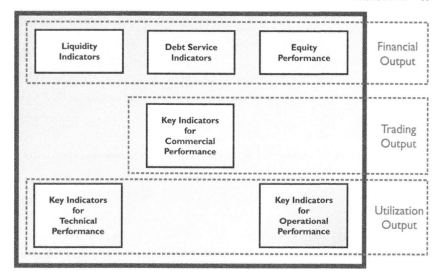

Figure 18.1 Fundamental content of a dashboard

Based on the priorities of the shipping company, a dashboard should visualize critical items and indicators from these departments and their operations. The fundamental content of a dashboard interface is illustrated in Figure 18.1. For easy recognition, all items are grouped according to three levels: financial output, trading output, and utilization output.

The priority levels provide a rough outline for the dashboard, although the scope of output and other details should be fine-tuned. Many managers can easily organize the major items, but they may have difficulty with classifications based on frequency, horizons, thresholds, and data benchmarks.

A dashboard also serves as a synchronization instrument between different levels of governance. A mid-level manager knows that the company's upper managers see the information on the dashboard. This provides an incentive to quickly deal with issues.

The appearance of dashboards is another less considered issue. The value of good visual design is immeasurable, even though it may seem like a costly detail. Well-designed visuals can improve the recognition of critical items and, in turn, improve the effectiveness of the tool. To illustrate how important visuals are, I designed the hypothetical dashboard in Figure 18.2. Some key figures and market data are presented at the top of the window and some financial indicators are on the top-right. As an example, some ships in the fleet are demonstrated in the main part of the window. On the left side there are the budget, the ship's current average speed with a long-term average, a port state control indicator, and fuel performance. Mid-ship are some financial figures. The scale on the cargo hold refers to the percentage loaded (L), discharged (D), or sailing (S). 'VIDLE' refers to a charter not yet fixed, as opposed to one that is ('VFIXED').

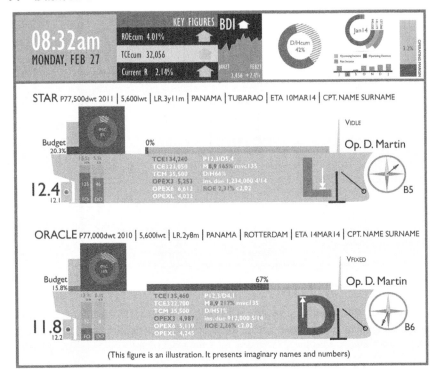

(This figure is an illustration. It presents imaginary names and numbers)

Figure 18.2 An example of a shipping company dashboard

Figure 18.2 is just an illustration of how a lot of data can be presented visually in a concise form. These visuals are related to the interface while the ANS-like procedures work in the background, executed by dedicated staff. The technology behind such ANS-like processes is an automated business management (ABM) system. For example, Microsoft Dynamics is one of the popular software solutions for such systems. An ABM system gathers data, analyzes it, and even makes estimations. Finally, it presents information by using reporting styles and dashboards specific to the user (e.g. one for the financial manager and another for the operational manager). KPIs play a significant role in the ABM system. Both KPIs and the financial indicators are frequently calculated and compared with industry benchmarks (e.g. an industry average). Machine learning can be well embedded in such systems.

By using an ABM system, top managers leave some tasks to automated processes that can even produce messages and alerts for low-ranking staff. The C-level executives just review the overall picture and respond to the automated signals.

19 The age of artificial intelligence
What computational intelligence needs to be

Knowledge gap • Neo-shipping economicus
Predictive analytics • Machine learning • Deep learning

An ordinary shipping professional has various questions about buzzwords such as digitalization, block chain, artificial intelligence and so on. The so-called technology boom of maritime industry is expected to change more or less everything from ships to some intellectual activities like forecasting or valuation. It is a common belief that we expect a new skill set (the new shipping man) to enter the industry during the first half of the 21st century: *the neo-shipping economicus*. In terms of some academic and intellectual skills, *neo-shipping economicus* (henceforth NSE) is completely different from an ordinary professional. NSE is expected to be knowledgeable enough to adapt to the age of artificial intelligence or, in other words, computational intelligence.

Computational intelligence has been utilized and applied in the financial markets by financial engineers for more than a decade, and there are already plenty of financial engineering firms throughout Manhattan using mathematical models (aka algorithmic trading) or machine learning. Some programming platforms such as R or Python are used to develop algorithms and generate business analytics without expert intervention. These days, even primary and secondary school kids learn to code in Python for some simple applications. Python is a coding platform with an increasing volume of use and applications in several areas. According to some recent statistics, it will be the top coding and programming platform for data scientists in the first half of this century (already preferred to some traditional platforms). So the NSE will probably need to understand the mechanism of coding and particularly Python programming in the near future.

The shipping industry is way behind what is going on in finance and banking (as of 2018). The knowledge gap will be reduced possibly in a few decades, but that will definitely require the NSE with some computing as well as mathematical skills. Currently, there is no educational institution which meets the requirements of both computational and industrial skills needed in the shipping business. Therefore, we may expect some new faces and specialties to join the industry and learn its dynamics. Recently, many shipping firms (operators, data vendors and so on) have invested significantly in manpower with computational skills. Some well-known firms have appointed their own innovation directors.

During such a historical shift in the industry, the ordinary shipping professional and shipping investor will suffer due to the knowledge gap and its management. Experts in machine learning have proposed various methodologies, and some investors spend in the region of US$30k–200k in establishing such complex systems. There is a widespread understanding that machine learning could result in extraordinary performance in market prediction. Without dedicating a massive budget, the performance of these systems cannot be tested, and therefore, there will be a time lag between spending and knowing the accuracy of systems. Unfortunately, there have been many disappointments due to various limitations of those systems or the lack of shipping industry and predictive analytics knowledge on the developers' side. I believe this knowledge gap between parties is a source of the "market for lemons" phenomenon for shipping investors and professionals. Even I experience such miscommunication in my research team composed of econometricians and electronic engineers. The traditional econometrics and the new computational approach each have their own technical jargons and different lenses for similar problems. As a professor, I am more of a translator than a leader in this puzzling circumstance. I can understand both parties in their own jargons, but it is difficult to maintain efficient communication between those distinct specialties.

***

Econometrics and one branch in particular, time series analysis, has a long history in economics, going back to the first half of the 1900s, and has been utilized in shipping market analysis for several decades. Market forecasts published by various shipping research firms are possibly developed using some form of econometric model. In the history of maritime economics research, econometrics has always been a powerful instrument with enormous persuasive power. One of the founding fathers of econometrics, Jan Tinbergen (1934), also studied modelling of the shipping freight market. Time series analysis fundamentally uses some form of curve-fitting on a given data set. There are hundreds of different methodologies in this particular stream of research for generating predictions in a spectrum of different horizons (short term vs. long term) or objectives (point vs. interval forecast, raw data vs. volatility forecasting). The International Institute of Forecasters[1] is currently the leading organization in forecasting research, and the vast majority of its members still employ econometric methodologies in predictive models.

In contrast to econometrics, computational intelligence and machine learning in specific has no such a long history, at least in business practice. Before going further, I should clarify terminology used interchangeably here. Artificial intelligence and computer intelligence broadly refer to the same concept. I prefer computational intelligence with its wider scope. Machine learning, artificial neural networks and its complex variant, deep learning, fall into the area of computational intelligence.

The big leap in computational intelligence in financial markets happened around 2000–2004. Early in the 2003–2008 economic boom, hundreds of financial engineering firms were established, and many of them are still active in the algorithmic trading business. Algorithmic trading refers to automated stock buy/sell systems based on some trading rules and predictive analytics. A computer-based trader replaces a real trader and performs all required operations in the stock market while collecting and compiling data streams to calibrate the decision-making program.

There is another reason for the development of machine learning in the last decade: big data. Systems sensing and collecting data have evolved through the 2000s (including social media), and firms have faced the challenge of using and utilizing the big data collected from various resources. In the shipping industry, ship position and movement data (i.e. AIS data) is a unique example of big data. How big is the big data? Roughly, it is expected to include millions of data points. When it comes to ship positions on a global scale, there are way more than a million data points in a month (if not in a week).

***

Machine learning and deep learning are some very cool methodologies with a lot of power in terms of pattern recognition and classification (e.g. face recognition). This kind of use of machine learning involves a 'matching' process in which the computer searches and matches given images within a pre-identified database (i.e. computer vision). This feature of machine learning is expected to replace the lookout officer/seaman someday. Some early versions of intelligent lookout systems are already being developed and will be installed in fully automated (also unmanned) ships. By using regular, infrared, or night-view cameras, those systems can achieve great performance even in some situations where the human eye is limited. Computer vision can be utilized for tracking a ship's radar echoes or detecting a watch-keeping officer at bridge.[2]

***

One of the biggest uses of machine learning is predictive analytics. This is also known as the 'black box' solution since the process of forecasting is not apparent to users of machine learning systems. Users briefly enter a bundle of data which is expected to have some explanatory power, then the system outputs a value for a projected future date. Different kinds of architectures can be developed and tested in a machine learning environment. In econometrics, it is very straightforward to find the impact of any particular variable and its significance. Machine learning is a completely other world and another way of 'extrapolating' for prediction. In this approach, some hidden relationships are found by a training procedure, and the final architecture is then reactivated to generate some future values by using new inputs to the system.

Good and bad uses of machine learning

Machine learning does not offer a magical wand that allows you to just enter all of your data and get amazing predictions. The vast majority of data scientists using machine learning do not really understand the mechanism behind the predictive process and usually confuse it with 'matching'-type applications. There is very solid evidence indicating that some traditional (and simpler) forecasting methodologies are still much more accurate in prediction than sophisticated approaches like machine learning. The number of data scientists who can really develop practically useful and meaningfully accurate predictive systems is very small. There are so many disappointing shipping business applications. Although companies have invested thousands and even tens of thousands of dollars in various sorts of machine learning systems, few of them actually work properly in terms of predictive analytics.

There are various reasons behind the failure of machine learning in shipping market prediction. I do not want to waste these pages with technical details, but the greatest problem in machine learning is the 'over-fitting' problem. Since machine learning uses so many layers and nodes, it can perfectly fit to any kind of data set which seems unbelievably accurate at the first place. However, those curve fits eventually fail in terms of generating accurate 'out of sample' forecasts (real business forecasting). There are some ways to deal with the problem, but these countermeasures are still relatively new ideas in the machine learning world. Unfortunately, many data scientists do not really follow the developments in this field.

How to spot a liar in predictive analytics?

I would like to share some brief strategies to test predictive systems and recognize the difference between computational garbage and computational intelligence. These are not a complete set of strict rules but more a rule of thumb to spot liars in this industry.

Naïve forecaster test

From time to time, I mention the 'naïve forecaster fallacy' at shipping events. A naïve forecaster thinks that tomorrow will be the same as today. For example, if the Panamax time charter daily rate is $11,000 today, the prediction of the naïve person for tomorrow would be exactly $11,000, no more no less. A slightly better naïve forecaster just copies trends. If the Panamax time charter rate was $10,000 yesterday, today's price corresponds to a 10% increase, and the naïve forecaster will expect $12,100 ($11,000 plus 10% of

$11,000) for tomorrow. The naïve forecaster always follows this basic principle. At the end of the day, the naïve forecaster only fails in determining turning points! During the rest of the time, predictions are always more or less accurate; at least their direction is right. Now consider providers of market predictions for the shipping industry: how many of them really do better than a naïve forecaster?

The naïve forecaster test is a powerful instrument to spot a predictive liar of any kind (not only in machine learning). Any predictive analysis must be better than a naïve forecast. That is the baseline for predictive accuracy. If a prediction cannot outperform the naïve benchmark, it is computational garbage!

Curve-fitting is not prediction

In most cases, a predictive platform is tested in some historical data. So, a proposed machine learning system is probably advertised based on its success in fitting historical data. Then, predictive accuracy is presented as the degree of curve fit, the gap between the fitted curve and the historical data set. As a fundamental rule, curve-fitting has very limited value in terms of predictive accuracy, regardless of the methodology used to fit the curve (e.g. machine learning, mathematical model). In the current technology, a perfect fit can be generated by using some mathematical operations.[3] However, while a curve fit can represent meaningful and repetitive patterns and oscillations of data, it can also imitate meaningless patterns and noise (random oscillations). Therefore, any methodology focusing on fitting a curve eventually fails in terms of prediction. This is the over-fitting problem which we have already mentioned in relation to good and bad uses of machine learning.

Predictive models must always be applied with some holdout sample which is not used for training and modelling. You may exclude some data from your sample and ask a prediction provider to generate forecasts for a holdout period. Then, you will be able to assess whether the proposed method really works in business practice.

Is it worth investing in a sophisticated one when a simple one works better?

In forecasting research, there are so many methodologies that stretch out econometrics to digital signal processing and other fractions of computational intelligence. In the last few decades, various forecasting competitions have been conducted by using thousands of different data sets (economic, transport, health, population, and so on) with different data frequencies (daily, weekly, monthly, annually). One common result of the competitions is that the simpler models usually outperform the complex ones. For example, Holt-Winters exponential smoothing works well in many of the data sets. This raises an impotant question: is it worth spending more for a sophisticated machine learning system? My answer is "it depends." If a prediction algorithm or system outperforms simpler and more conventional methodologies, it is worth investing. Otherwise, once again, it is computational garbage.

***

In my research team, our motto is 'first outperform the naïve forecaster.' A predictive model must first outrank naïve forecast. Your predictive analytics are actually as strong as your benchmarks. Based on this, we developed the Intelligent Model Search Engine (IMSE) in early 2018 and presented our initial results at the Singapore Exchange (SGX) to a group of professionals in the shipping and commodity markets. The IMSE is a kind of Google for prediction modeling which follows a certain testing and modelling procedure, ensuring its accuracy against all conventional methodologies in tough market conditions. It is a fair forecasting contest without any prior assumptions on which models would predict better. To be honest, even the most accurate configuration changes through time and at various stages of the market. Therefore, the search for the best model is a never-ending, recursive procedure.

Notes

1　https://forecasters.org/.
2　A significant proportion of ship accidents are caused by sleeping or unconscious watch-keeping officers.
3　For example, time-frequency representations can be used to extract the perfect curve, fitting data completely.

20 Lenders' stimulus
Even bankers can be misled

Ship finance • *Shipping banks*
Adverse motivations • *Confirmation bias*

Financial symbols, particularly the ones representing money itself, prime our selfish motives, as behavioral economics and neuroeconomics have found. The word 'selfish' itself is usually upsetting, and few people have any good sentiments when they encounter the term. However, classical economics assume that people are rational decision-makers—that is, rationally selfish.

When I first studied the connection between symbols for currency and how they automatically trigger selfish behavior and thoughts, I began thinking about how difficult bankers' lives must be. They are surrounded by such symbols for most of their lives. Accordingly, they should be the most selfish people in the world. My experience, and that of my colleagues, confirms this suspicion: many people who work with and/or manage money for a living (e.g. accountants) tend to be ungenerous, close-fisted, and highly skeptical. (This last trait is probably a good one.) They are probably not inherently selfish, but the cognitive bias of their profession pushes them in this direction. Also, they are trained to see the risks in every proposition. When we are considering the risky business of shipping, the nature of the work requires them to refine these traits.

Shipping finance

A long time ago, I was seated in the room of a finance professor talking to his colleague who occasionally mentioned shipping matters. The professor turned to me and began to talk about his interest in shipping finance. As a young researcher, he had attempted to study the subject. It was very difficult for him because of the array of technical matters with tankers, bulk carriers, ports, flag states, special covenants, etc.

Financing ships is probably the most specialized sector in the world of banking and finance. That is why we have specialized shipping banks. They deal with globally mobile vehicles and their related offshore companies. Here, the tangible assets are less important than the intangible ones: profession, reputation, and a good sense of the dynamics of the shipping business.

There are many good stories—as well as bad ones—in shipping finance. Take foreclosures, for instance. Taking money back is sensitive work. When it comes to our industry, we have two safeguards: collateral (e.g. ships, other assets) and monitoring tools (e.g. liquidity, minimum value, debt-to-hull ratio). Conventional banks cannot handle managing a ship after a foreclosure, properly valuing shipping assets, or the high level of mobility. However, shipping banks or banks with specialized shipping departments can.

In the last few decades, shipping finance has become more sophisticated. Monitoring shipping loans is easier with expertise. There are more intermediaries facilitating ship financing. Newcomers to the industry in particular need a facilitating agent who can teach them and convert their needs into what shipping bankers want to hear. Shipping finance has its own terminology and methods. Good communication is essential; therefore, you need somebody who can speak the language. Moreover, these intermediaries must know how to deal with the incentives of bankers.

If you want to understand somebody, you should know about what drives them. Think back to our discussion on representation: the right kind leads to good deals and less risk premiums. Bankers want to know how risky you are. If you are not overly risky, you may have a deal. If you are a minimal risk, you may have a good deal. If you are a newcomer and want a good deal, though, you must have a facilitator. The perceptions of bankers vary, but they seem to be related to the state of the shipping market. Shipping bankers want to make deals with shipowners who have a strong balance sheet and a high level of liquidity.

Stimulus

Shipping banks have developed new systems, procedures, policies, and models. They have dedicated staff who are more like scholars than traditional bankers. When everything is going well and the market is at a peak, lenders tend to finance easily, and vice versa. I do not completely understand their behavior. When everything goes badly and the market is in a recession, the situation cannot be worse—it has already reached the bottom. If a shipowner can rationally invest in bad times, this should be less risky for a financier. However, they usually tend to support the industry in a bull market rather a bear market.

The lenders' case is a little bit different. Collateral, covenants, and the financial engineering product of security bonds work for lenders. Lenders finance and share their risk with risk-seeking investors in the bond market (i.e. collateralized debt obligations, or CDOs). Although the security bond solution causes a loss of credit rating for them, it is a way of transferring the risk. The relationship between shipowners and lenders is somewhat like supply and demand in economics, but there is also a give-and-take dimension in terms of behavioral economics. During a peak market, shipowners look for evidence to rationalize their actions (supported by an abundance of cash), and lenders are there, waiting to enable their decisions. Since their intention is to lend, they may play into the confirmation bias by lending the shipowner money for whatever investment or project they have in mind. This can signal to the shipowner that, yes, they are making a good decision—why else would the bank lend them money? Just remember: thinking critically about long-term success is the responsibility of the shipowner, not their banker.

21 The magic of the discount factor
Temporal myopia and hyperbolic discounting

Discounted cash flow • Forecasting
Temporal myopia • Time assumption • Hyperbolic discounting

In the history of mankind, a piece of paper could not change one's life so much as money could. Ironically, there is nothing behind the value of money today. A long time ago, paper money was a kind of certificate representing an amount of gold in the bank. It had a specific value. Today, though, we just carry these pieces of paper around without any sense of tangible value. The story of money is divided into two ages: before Bretton Woods and after. Before the conference at Bretton Woods, you could exchange your paper currency for gold. After Bretton Woods, money was no longer linked to gold. It is a commodity itself with its value determined by the supply and demand for it.

One of the results of this change is the difficulty in recognizing the value of money, especially in regards to time. If you know the historical prices of basic commodities, then you may calculate the change in value. But, we rarely know the valuation for money itself. It is not constant through time. It fluctuates, like the purchasing power of a dollar in the 1990s not being the same as it is today.

A shipping investor needs a business plan and a feasibility study for an intended ship project. A feasibility study tells of the financial future of the project and its cash flow estimations. The most complicated task is determining the financial future. The future value of money changes according to random variables, the unpredictability of the market, and the sporadic nature of currency policy. But before discussing this, I want to talk about the future itself.

The science of the future

People want to know their own future as well as the future of mankind. Talking about the future is historically valued. Take Nostradamus: every sporadic event, global crisis, and political debate is linked to him and his predictions of the future. Today, dealing with the future is a scientific field. Forecasting is popular in terms of financial, economic, social, and even political purposes. For instance, several studies dealing with the U.S. presidential elections have shown that body language, word choice, slogans, and so on can be indicative of future victory.

In finance, forecasting is usually achieved through econometrics or time series analyses. State-of-the-art software exists that can estimate models and generate predictions. Although such methods and models are well known, we still need expert help in finding the right one.

In the science of forecasting, there are many methods for a variety of purposes. They are primarily divided into two groups: quantitative and qualitative methods. Quantitative methods take a picture of the past and then extrapolate it to the future. The important thing is how it is extrapolated. The traditional approach uses historical data, finds a trend, and then assumes the trend will continue. In the case of qualitative methods, a number of experts are asked to forecast the future, based on their experience and/or past data.

Regardless, the crucial question is how to validate your method. You have to check whether it works and predicts accurately. I have spent a long time in forecasting science and reviewed many academic papers developing models and extrapolating predictions. I can say that roughly 90% of all academic efforts with forecasting (both published and unpublished) are invalid. The reason is that many of them do not employ an out-of-sample control (Figure 21.1), they do not use proper accuracy metrics, and—like shipowners—scientists are humans with strong rationalization powers. We have our own confirmatory processes, and the statistics are flexible enough to allow for moral hazard and adverse selection.

For example, you need some benchmark methods to compare your results against. This way, you will validate or invalidate your approach. The problem is that the selection of benchmark methods is subjective. If I put an inferior method against my method, of course my method will be superior. We use the term 'validation'—and we scientists really work to make our results live up to the name. Really, we should use the term 'falsification.' That would be a more honest and meaningful term.

There are strong methods for forecasting some kinds of data (but not all), but they need expertise, criticism, and effective falsification control. We usually tend to confirm something. Sometimes it needs to be falsified to find a solution that works in practice.

Spreadsheets and real life

Investment analyses and the control of financial indicators need some calculations and estimations. A shipping investor first needs a clear objective of profitability and maybe some thresholds for particular actions (e.g. stay, quit,

Figure 21.1 Definition of the out-of-sample period in historical data

size-up). For example, a threshold of return on equity (ROE) could be useful in their future assessments.

After we clarify our financial objectives, we need to identify the future of the intended project. We begin with some assumptions and estimations of the operation period, costs, revenues, interest rates, etc. Then we put this into spreadsheets, including the cash flows for the project's lifespan. Finally, we need the value of the project in terms of today's purchasing power. We know that ten years from today one dollar will not be the same as it is now. The conventional method for project valuation is the DCF analysis (or net present value analysis). For this, we discount each cash flow entry from the time of realization to the present. To do so, we need a number called a discount factor. This serves as a proxy for the inflation rate.

In 1996, Laverty performed an interesting study to find the impact of the discount factor and net present value calculations. As illustration, he used two projections. One was a less risky project with long-term, positive cash flows and the other was a risky project (e.g. a new technology) with negative cash flows in the short term but strong, positive cash flows in the long term (Laverty, 1996). In Figure 21.2, project A is the less risky one and project B is the more risky one. If we use a discount factor of over 2%, then we find that project A is superior to project B. However, it is clear that project B earns much more than project A in the long term and that its future is quite bright. This is what I call the magic of the discount factor.

If a shipping investor deals with these financial reports, nobody recognizes the magic unless there is a huge gap between projects. The discount factor can easily mislead decision-makers, particularly when the numbers are very close.

In closing this chapter, I need to address a practical reality. A spreadsheet does not show you what happens on board, at port, at the time of major company inspections, etc. Assumptions should include failures, ship detentions, and other unexpected operations events. When spreadsheets look perfect, they are self-serving and confirmatory instruments that just rationalize our intentions. It does not show what we should be looking for. In addition, if our actions are not based on the plan, then the spreadsheets are worth nothing.

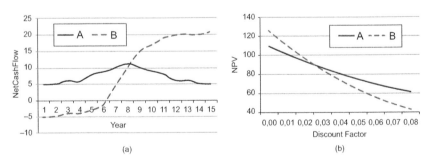

Figure 21.2 The net cash flow diagram of project A and project B (a) and their NPV results (b)

22 Credit engineering
Misleading habits

Liquidity engineering • *Lending push*
Probability engineering • *Liquidity cycle*

I have learned many lessons from grocery shopping. Akerlof's (1978) "markets for lemons" is not the only a simple example of the tricky world of economics. There are many other misleading practices. Like many other people, I like apples—especially red, shiny ones. However, you may have noticed that these apples are somewhat oily. The produce staff or the wholesaler performs a varnishing process before putting them on display—but we shoppers see only a shiny, red apple. We buy it, eat it, and get a small dopamine reward for the experience, thus creating a habit triggered by the sheen. Companies want to create habits that sell more products. People are primed to consume certain drinks for gastrointestinal health or capsules for weight loss, etc. Once the habits are established, it is like turning on an autonomous consumption engine. Neuromarketing is a topic with growing interest, particularly in the research centers of private companies.

People consume several tangible products, like food, cars, or clothing, but also intangibles, like trends, philosophies, models, and thoughts. The same rules work here too: once a habit is established, it is like an autonomous consumption engine. The average person does not criticize or rethink their habits and does not care about prior conditions. The financial world is full of such intangible products, like numbers, functions, and sophisticated models. Experts use these instruments without reserve and sometimes cannot avoid jumping on the bandwagon based on the incentives behind the system.

In financial assessments and mathematical statistics, there have been many complicated methods and models developed in the last few decades. There are also some traditional approaches like the DCF method. That magical number, the discount factor, plays a significant role in such analyses. The discount factor usually defines whether or not a project is feasible. The size of the discount factor is frequently defined using a risk-free interest rate, such as the one provided by Treasury bills or the London InterBank Offer Rate (LIBOR). Since the discount factor has a serious impact on the outcome of an analysis, you should be aware of the dynamics behind the interest rates. I should highlight the recent LIBOR scandal due to fraudulent activities and manipulation of LIBOR rates. Several banks were fined due to their role in manipulation and submission of biased interest rates. As a consequence of the scandal, the U.K. Financial Conduct Authority (FCA) announced plans to replace the LIBOR with an alternative by 2021.[1]

Producing feasibility

Central banks manage liquidity with monetary policy instruments. The most important is the rate for their funds that guides short-term interest rates. The U.S. Federal Reserve also uses open market operations to affect Treasury bond yields. When interest rates are low, capital is easily available. Low rates reduce the risk of borrowing because the return only has to be higher than the interest rate. This makes more investments look feasible. By producing feasibility, liquidity creates economic growth.

At the beginning of 2007, the U.S. Federal Reserve decided to reduce interest rates dramatically. After a few months, LIBOR also declined enormously, while other leading economies, such as in the U.K., Japan, and the Eurozone, kept the rates as they were (higher than their average; see Figure 22.1). The lax interest rate policy of the U.S. Federal Reserve has several influences—explicit and implicit, direct and indirect. As a result of the process, an artificial liquidity boom was primed as a byproduct of 'liquidity engineering' (Figure 22.1).

For the vast majority of the world, this was an amazing decision that would lead to a high rate of credit expansion. Since interest rates were low, it would seem to be a good time for massive market entries in addition to the rationalization of project feasibilities. Once the interest rates were reduced, the discount factor declined and the net present value of future cash flows settled at a reasonable level. Therefore, many investment projects became feasible by utilizing interest rate instruments. One of the most essential habits of financial decision-makers is the unique discounting process. As I discussed previously, money cannot preserve its value over time. It loses value day by day. The discounting routine is reasonable and useful from the standpoint of diminishing value. However, a decision-maker still needs an accurate and credible estimation of the discount factor for making sound calculations. An average interest rate over a number of years may be used as an estimation for a discount factor. It is obvious that there is no strict standard for defining the discount factor. If a lender really intends to raise funds for you, then the discount factor can be somewhat adjusted. For example, the length of historical data can be shortened to benefit from the recent decline in interest rates. But why do lenders tend to relax their funds, and what are their motivations for doing so?

Revision of the discount factor is not the only thing to impact interest rates. Since a Treasury bill does not earn much, lenders tend to increase their credit businesses and take on more risks to ensure their return objectives. In addition to that, regional or national banks can find cheaper, syndicated funds from global lenders and can sell these funds to local customers at a premium.

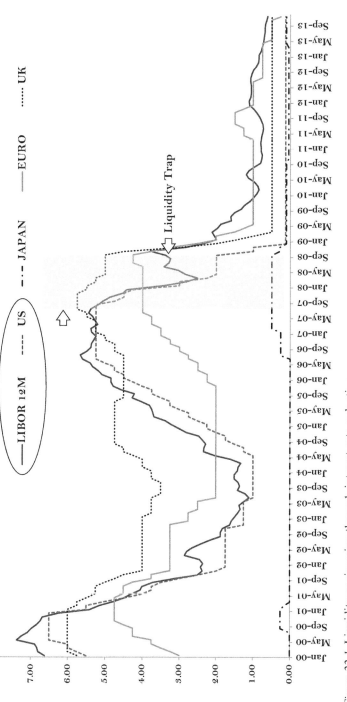

Figure 22.1 Liquidity engineering through interest rate reduction

As a result, liquidity engineering creates an optimistic climate and an incentive to lend.

With liquidity engineering, lenders are surrounded with a strong, optimistic climate. Their bonus system may motivate experts to create some loan transactions with more risk. Now we add one more factor: the powerful bonus/commission incentive. But there are still other dimensions absent from this story.

Probability engineering

One of the most famous mathematicians in history is Bayes, father of the Bayesian probability rules. The theories of Bayes laid the groundwork for modern risk assessment. Let's say there are ten instances that result in two bad outcomes; we would probably conclude that there is a 20% probability of a bad outcome next time. If there are two consecutive processes with the same probability of a bad outcome, their cumulative probability is $0.20 \times 0.20 = 0.04$, or 4%. In the case of a coin toss, there is a 50% probability of throwing heads and a 50% probability of tails. These are simple calculations, but the case is not so simple in human-based complex systems—particularly with our economic decisions.

In using past (i.e. historical) data, I am quite skeptical. My reason is the uncertainty of the optimal scope of historical data for deriving trends. In Figure 22.2 there are a series of hypothetical data. If I want to produce a probability distribution of this data set to use in risk assessment, I must select a sample (i.e. length of historical data, sample size) for an estimation).

To ensure fairness, my heart says you should use the entire data set. To ensure an up-to-date outcome and to eliminate the impact of inflation or any other long-term trends (e.g. a change in technology), my brain says you should use more recent data. However, *sample A* produces significantly higher outcomes than *sample B*. Since the average levels of data increase according to the sample, the difference in results will be dramatic. Let's assume this data is based on revenues from the shipping business (i.e. freight rate income). By shifting between these samples, I can take different pictures of revenue probabilities. Adding different data points skews the average, and this could be used to rationalize a risky project.

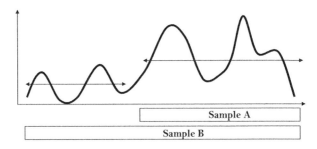

Figure 22.2 Subjectivity in sample selection for risk assessment

Ignoring the tricky particulars of such methods causes risky transactions. From another perspective, such methods can produce excuses for improper risk assessment. It is not that experts execute these analyses improperly so much as the conventionally accepted methods work improperly. There is a

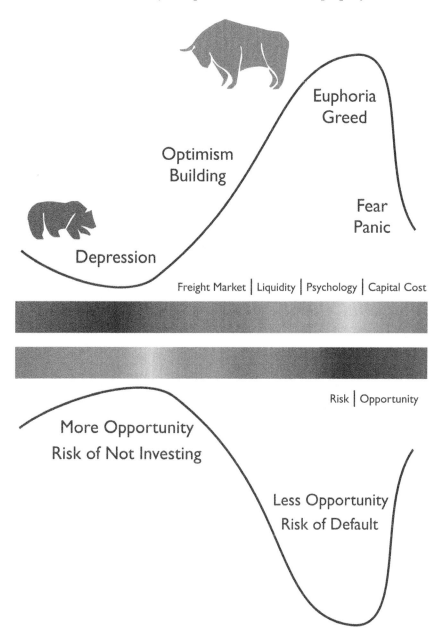

Figure 22.3 Cycles of liquidity, mood, and risk

simple reason for failure: since experts want a good outcome, the method delivers it. Have you ever read *How to Lie with Statistics* by Darrell Huff? In it, he shares how anyone can find the subjective side of statistics and the instruments with which statistical evidence can be manipulated. In his own words: "The crooks already know these tricks; honest men must learn them in self-defense" (Huff, 1993, p. 11).

Liquidity, mood, and risk

After discussing liquidity engineering, I must mention liquidity cycles. As we examined earlier, a typical business cycle is divided into four periods: trough, recovery, peak, and decline (Figure 22.3). This has parallels with a behavioral perspective: depression = recession; optimism = hope; euphoria = excitement and greed; and finally fear = panic. Investors' livelihoods tend to correlate with liquidity cycles: poverty, enrichment, abundance, and impoverishment.

However, the cycle of risk and profitable opportunities is almost the opposite of liquidity or liquidity-based mood cycles. Any simple feasibility study shows that prospering in the shipping business is strongly correlated with asymmetric investments. During recessions, ships are quite cheap and interest rates are very low, while the freight market is very low. During market highs, ships are overvalued and interest rates are very high, while the freight market is optimistic from the shipowners' standpoint. Shipping investors who can maintain liquidity through the depression (if patient enough to do so) may benefit from cheaper shipping assets and asset play. Liquidity engineering is a way of wiping out the cash generated through the cycle. Once you lose your liquidity and strong balance sheet, you lose the opportunity to benefit from the following recession. By losing liquidity control, asset play will be a theoretical exercise rather than a practical outcome. Every shipowner tells the same story: buy cheap, sell high, and win in asset play. However, few of them can put theory into practice. Most of them still believe that they can detect the turning point so there is no need for alarm. Almost nobody can detect the turning point a couple of months before prices begin declining. Therefore, waiting for the turning point is probably not a good strategy.

Note

1   Further details may be found at https://en.wikipedia.org/wiki/Libor_scandal.

23 Risk vs. uncertainty
Swine flu and shipping

Risk perception • Liquidity risk
Monte Carlo simulations • Subjectivity of
risk assessments

The year 2009 was extraordinary. The Air France flight 447 crashed with 228 souls on board, the U.S. elected its first African-American president, General Motors and Chrysler declared bankruptcy, and the Lakers beat Orlando Magic. There is one more important event we should remember: the swine flu pandemic with its ensuing mania. By mid-2009, swine flu was seen as a serious global problem. At the time, we read about it every day. The news reported that some people even died. From media accounts, it was clear that the swine flu pandemic was unusual (i.e. "This time, it's different!"). The prevalence of swine flu and the risks from it seemed higher than our historical perception of it. While it was indeed a concern, there was no statistical evidence of an unusual development or higher than normal mortality rates. In fact, the mortality was less than in some previous years. The World Health Organization has been reprimanded for creating a 'false pandemic' and for alleged unethical cooperation with pharmaceutical firms. If this had been the case, it would be one of the greatest medicine scandals in history: over 65 million vaccine doses were consumed during the scare. However, there are some lessons to be learned in understanding how risk affects the cognitive self.

The first lesson concerns the statistics behind the risk. Using and finding numbers to represent risk can be misguided by uncertain data and, particularly, the emotional perception of risk. Almost all of the numerical methods of statistics depend on the researcher's expertise and have an element of moral hazard. When emotions take control, the statistics may tell you what you want to hear. The swine flu mania illustrates how a common statistical fact can be perceived as an unusual health risk and go on to spark a global panic. The seasonal flu causes deaths all over world, particularly in underdeveloped areas. While unfortunate, this is common. The difference between seasonal flu and swine flu is that the mortality statistics of the former rarely become a global debate. When the mortality statistics of the swine flu hit newspaper headlines, there was an unusually keen interest in the data. The previously little-known data became public knowledge overnight. There is a strong need for critical and objective judgment on the selection of risk factors as well as the associated data regarding exposure and frequency. The recency bias works well in such a context. People tend to deal with current numbers. In the shipping business, exaggerated pricing is common and the economic history of shipping records many instances of it. The booms of the swine flu and shipping assets may have equivalent factors behind them, with a pandemic (i.e. strong pessimism) boosting the perception of a health risk, in contrast to shipping booms (i.e. strong optimism) that dramatically reduce our perception of risk exposure.

The second lesson concerns the mystery of the sporadic and unknown. At the beginning of the pandemic, the swine flu was classified as an extraordinary virus similar to the 1918 outbreak of Spanish flu that killed an estimated 40 million people. This was an outlier since there was a 91-year gap.

These two dimensions make it difficult to properly assess current risk. Likewise, when the reason behind a shipping boom is uncertain, similar principles hide the basis for recognizing the context, background, analogies, gap between the past and present, and dynamics of the business. In the case of the swine flu, experts should note the gap between 1918 and 2009 in terms of the histology, hygiene, technology, quality of health services, and advances in drug research, among other factors, while keeping in mind the unexceptional characteristics of the seasonal flu for so many years in history. In the case of shipping booms, we should note the impossibility of an unending demand as well as the nature of cycles, having a gradually increasing trend and a sharp market crash. We will probably never see a different picture (a sharp uptick followed by a gradual drop). Any sporadic or unexpected boom, uncertain growth, or historically unusual period of prosperity will finally come to a conclusion. History may not reveal the exact numbers relating to these trends, but it does show us what the dynamics of herd behavior are. Uncertainty makes us blind and drunk—we may suddenly become either depressed or euphoric, losing our ability to objectively assess risk.

The perception of risk and the actual level of risk may be quite different. Sometimes, we heuristically measure risk to be high, while it is very low in reality. If we compare the risk factor with others that we classify as low risk, we may find them similar or even identical. For example, it is very common to be pessimistic during times of recession. Shipping investors tend to have a high-risk perception of the market. However, shipping markets have already reached a great low when the economy is in a recession. Therefore, an upturn, or higher rates, is more likely than additional decline when in a deep market.

This is very similar to the risk perception of swine flu. People thought that there was a high risk of a harmful pandemic and mortality, whereas the actual risk was low. Human beings have emotions that play a significant role in the risk evaluation process. Our emotions can amplify our perceptions of either the exposure to or frequency of perceived risk.

Since our emotions are strongly linked with our personalities and cultural values, geographic locations may also have an influence in the perception of risk. Some of us are more sensitive and would even like to achieve zero risk. For example, the use of face masks is very common in various Asian countries even in a common seasonal flu.

Some people are so risk-averse as to seek risk-free investments, sacrificing opportunities and marginal gains. On the other hand, some of us are risk-seekers who tend to choose opportunities despite uncertainties and volatility. It is quite difficult to assess the superiority of either of these extremes.

The approach of Japanese shipping firms is mostly based on risk-free (or very low risk) business, that makes it the superior choice for a time horizon of decades or even centuries. On the opposite side, we have many disappointing stories of risk-seekers in the shipping business. It seems that the governance of risk is one of the most influential factors of success in the shipping business. With less subjectivity and a powerful risk monitoring system, reasonable exposure to risk may contribute to benefiting from opportunities so long as the predefined risk thresholds are not exceeded. The critical questions concern what the reasonable risk is and how to recognize it.

Dimensions of risk

Assessing risk is a difficult task since it requires several estimations and predictions as well as a number of assumptions. Although it is not a painful procedure to perform a risk assessment on paper, it may be impractical and/or represent more of a perfection of conditions. The traditional dimensions of risk are the volume of exposure (impact) and the frequency of the event that is assumed to be risky (harmful).

Risk of an undesired event = exposure (size of impact) × frequency (repetition)

With shipping investments, there are a number of challenges such as default risk (e.g. credit default, business default/bankruptcy) and liquidity risk (e.g. instant decline of working capital, which terminates the operation of ships). The exposure to these risk factors is closely related with the state of the shipping markets.

When the freight market is in recession, rates are already very low. Therefore, there is no extreme probability of further decline. This means the exposure of the default risk or liquidity risk is limited. On the other hand, the frequency of credit defaults and liquidity problems is high. Recessions wipe out many companies before the subsequent recovery of the market.

In contrast to recession, a market's peak means there is a probability of default and liquidity risk. Since the history of shipping has a vast number of unexpected sharp declines and market crashes, a peak market means that a great loss (e.g. value of ships, freight rates, stock prices, etc.) may arise suddenly, with part of the reason being triggering of fear.

Based on the trade-off between dealing with exposure or frequency, a shipowner needs to define a pathway that addresses some of these risks while ensuring safeguards for eliminating business defaults.

Liquidity risk

The economic climate, such as a high or a trough, is related to the average 'temperature' of money. In the summer (i.e. prosperity), money is very hot and passes through many different accounts and hands. There is an extremely high speed of money circulation, with consumers spending it without any hesitation or fear. Since the speed of money is quite high, the summer of economics is like a liquidity festival. Nobody worries about short-term debt.

When the economic climate turns to winter, the liquidity of the markets (i.e. the speed of money) sharply declines. People begin to worry about their cash flow and their short-term debt accordingly. The money chain is broken by delays on the collection of accounts receivable, and the capacity of working capital decreases. Finally, the liquidity crises hit the repayment of liabilities, leading to legal disputes, foreclosures, or bankruptcies.

Liquidity risk refers to the undesirable shortage of cash such that the firm becomes insolvent, unable to meet financial obligations. Therefore, the economic winter of the shipping recession is a kind of survival test for many shipping firms. The most critical characteristic of a strong balance sheet is a sustainable and robust liquidity. Before beginning a shipping project, every investor should seriously consider the sustainability of the prospective liquidity. Since ships are not secured assets (relative to other forms of assets) and shipping companies work in an offshore environment, the stakeholders of this industry are rarely patient enough for delayed repayments, especially when the investor is small and has only a few ships in their portfolio. Because shipping is a service industry, there is no inventory to liquidate in order to pay off debt. Therefore, liquidity defines the future of the investment in many cases.

The dramatic termination of prosperity is usually followed by a great decline of liquidity. When fear grips the market, the first effects are seen with short-term liabilities. To deal with it, decision-makers quickly turn to their liquidity monitoring instruments. There are two common metrics of the liquidity of a firm: the current ratio and the quick ratio (i.e. acid test ratio). The current ratio tells us the power of current assets to meet maturing short-term obligations (i.e. liabilities).

Current ratio = current assets/current liabilities

In addition to that, the quick ratio tells us the short-term repayment ability by excluding the inventories.

Quick ratio = cash and accounts receivable/current liabilities

However, we know that the inventory of a shipping firm is almost negligible. In this case, the current ratio roughly equals the quick ratio. The liquidity metrics should be major instruments in the dashboard of a shipping firm. They should be frequently reviewed, investigated, and questioned. The average current ratio of the shipping industry is around 2.0. For container and tanker shipping, it is slightly less than 2.0; perhaps 1.7. In dry bulk shipping, average current ratio is around 2.5. Industrial averages are useful for financial risk management. A shipping company should meet at least the industry average, but it should also improve over time.

For risk assessment, we need some predictions for operating revenue based on freight rates and liabilities (tied to interest rates). Then we can perform some simulations of possible liquidity outcomes and look at the percentage of undesired results. Similar simulations are also needed for analyzing turnover ratios (e.g. working capital turnover) and working capital (WC). A WC analysis is of more interest to managing directors than lenders. Lenders prefer to investigate cash flow statements. There may be two kinds of WC formulations, and both arrive at the same result.

WC = current assets − current liabilities (traditional WC function)

WC = fixed liabilities + equity − fixed assets

The first formula tells the story by using short-term indicators, while the second uses long-term indicators. The first is the conventional definition of WC, while the second is derived from the major components of the balance sheet (assets = liabilities + equity). The objective of the second formula is to investigate the source of WC or the use of it in the long term. Although the first formula is the traditional definition of WC, the second formula has practical merits that expose whether the liquidity problems are structural or temporary.

A liquidity risk assessment requires quality data, credible predictions, and state-of-the-art simulations for liquidity ratios and WC.

Self-serving simulations

In the case of lending proposals, lenders perform critical and skeptical analyses of prospective financial statements. This is a fairly common task of financial directors and key decision-makers in a firm. Therefore, simulations for financial results that include liquidity indicators should be performed frequently to detect current and upcoming problems. On the other hand, self-criticism is sometimes difficult for these people. Short-term incentives and impatient capital create a kind of intentional blindness to long-term prosperity. Short-term results are preferred at the expense of long-term loss.

The term 'Monte Carlo simulation' is frequently used to explain a simulation based on probability distributions of various data sets (e.g. revenues and costs). The basic difference between regular simulations and a Monte Carlo is the stochastic process that makes it somewhat subjective. Let me clarify this with an example. In fair-weather conditions, we may estimate the impact of a ship's propeller at a particular turning speed. Since engineers know the physical dynamics of seawater as well as those of the propeller, they can develop computer simulations to see the impact of the propeller without actually building it. The inputs, outputs, and environment for processing can be formulated and calculated precisely. The system works with the same principles that result in the same outputs. This is a deterministic simulation in contrast to a stochastic one. In the business environment, human action creates complexity and sometimes makes the outcome difficult to predict. Stochastic financial simulations use the gambling metaphor to illustrate uncertainty, complexity, and unpredictability.

We need a series of subjective selections of assumptions, prediction methods, inputs, and even data characteristics in a Monte Carlo simulation. Although the simulation is preferred, in the first place, over the judgmental predictions of experts, it still needs expert intervention. If a simulation is based on subjective selections, it is not surprising that moral hazard can work here as well. Monte Carlo simulations are exposed to self-serving bias, dishonesty, adverse selection, and many other cognitive biases of daily life. Monte Carlo simulation is still a popular topic in scientific research, though it is not yet a fully developed one. There are some procedures, but in many aspects, there are no standards. It is not an exaggeration to say that financial simulations may serve as the puppets of some decision-makers. These simulations tell them what they want to hear.

If shipowners tend to look at short-term figures and demand profits with a short-term focus, then it is not surprising that the managing directors supply figures that deliver on the owners' desired results. From this perspective, financial simulations may represent spurious works of art rather than the critical monitoring of a firm. For example, a simulation needs historical data. You can find 50-year-old data for time charter rates, but what is the proper way to select the data? Do you use the entire data set or select a section of it? Which one is better: 10 years of data or 20? Are there any standard rules or procedures about this selection, or is it a subjective process? Answering the last question will give you all you need: if there are no rules, it is absolutely subjective. If you define the length of data as ten years, then you assume that a ten-year data set is long enough to capture the cyclical behavior of the market while short enough to account for recent developments that would affect the long-term trend.

***

Risk and uncertainty are frequently used in the same context, sometimes even interchangeably. However, there is a small but significant difference between them. Risk refers to the occurrence probability of an undesired event. The term 'probability' should be noted. When we are talking about the probability, it means there is a measurable component. For example, probabilities can be calculated for rolling a dice or a coin toss. In financial analyses, experts are required to calculate probabilities of uncertainty for completing a risk assessment. For liquidity risk assessment, experts are required to calculate the probability of, for example, current liabilities greater than current assets (current ratio below 1.0). However, they are unable to calculate the uncertainty of the freight market as an input of current assets. Processing uncertainties is the key problem in modern business governance. Most of the existing financial education programs teach participants how to calculate probabilities for uncertainty and how to ignore the fact that uncertainty has no deterministic rules. Nobody can ignore the cyclic behavior of shipping markets, but people ignore the complexity and difficulty of calculating probabilities.

Optimistic pessimism

The essential reason of risk assessment is the possibility of default or, in other words, bankruptcy. In the shipping business, ships are usually registered under one-ship companies. Therefore, a default on a ship project does not always mean the complete bankruptcy of the shipping investor. However, a credit default may have harmful impacts on the investor in addition to an undermined reputation. Reduced liquidity is the leading signal of a default risk. Both liquidity and default risk analysis need scenario-based assessments that consist of pessimistic, moderate (i.e. reasonable), and optimistic scenarios. There are a number of problems with the characteristics of these scenarios. The most critical problem is with the optimistic or pessimistic scenario. If an optimistic scenario illustrates the levels of historical peaks, the pessimistic scenario should address the historical recessions. However, it is common to have a form of 'optimistic pessimism' in which even the pessimistic scenario is optimistic enough. Under the optimism bias, scenario analysis has no practical value. It is still a rationalization instrument.

If you really want to be critical about your prospective project, ignore the optimistic scenario and reduce the revenues of your pessimistic scenario about 20%. You will have two scenarios remaining: the reasonable scenario (aka the new optimistic scenario) and the recession scenario (aka the adjusted pessimistic scenario). It is a simple rule that gives you an opportunity for self-critique and in-depth analysis of what you are investigating. If you are a risk-averse investor, then completely ignore the reasonable scenario and just focus on the others. If you are confident about surviving in a recessionary period, you will not regret going into the shipping business.

Concluding remarks

Time is probably much more valuable now than in any other period of history. The advent of new technologies, particularly in communication and sharing knowledge, has created an ecosystem where only professionals using their time intelligently survive and prosper given today's speed of thought and action. The structure and content of this book is definitely extraordinary. Considering its objective and the volume of topics, I designed the chapters to be concise so that the reader could grab ideas as quickly as possible and save their valuable time.

In the shipping business, there are some fundamental problems that cause confusion and bias as well as representing a kind of orthodoxy. Our current knowledge, inherited from the research and practice of the last century, comprises many biased arguments and interpretations. For example, we discussed the origin of measurement for supply and demand in the shipping services (non-storable, non-transferable transportation space) in Chapter 2. Invention of the ton-mile metric goes back to the last century, and its application as shipping demand is an established norm of the industry. An experienced shipping analyst would know that seaborne trade volume has limited information about the direction of freight markets (it is a gradually increasing and relatively smooth data series). Most industrial research focuses on the supply side, which is thought to be the essential driver of shipping freight markets. In today's technology (e.g. AIS), more precise calculations of supply can be generated.

Another critical problem is the availability and quality of maritime data. As we discussed various cases in Chapters 4, 10, 21, and 22, maritime data is one of the biggest challenges for the industry. There are differences between data vendors, and some data sets are based on assessments instead of real transactions (e.g. freight indices when there is no transaction or negligible volume). Procedures employed in generating representative numbers are not clearly disclosed, and sometimes doubtful numbers are presented. Transaction data (fixtures) is incomplete or biased (e.g. sale price of ships). Since there are no clearing houses or exchange markets in the vast majority of those transactions, results are not as transparent as in a stock market (e.g. tick data).

Last but not least, ethical problems are rampant. Almost every professional in the shipping business frequently experiences unethical and unprofessional practices. There are so many incentives for people around a shipping firm or for shipping investors to cheat or lie or act in other unethical ways. Incentives are mostly mis-specified and not corrected properly. Many other industries have set regulations against practices that can cause massive failures. For example, the Financial Services Authority of the U.K. banned commission-based payments to investment advisers.[1] The reason behind this regulation comes from the fact that higher stock prices correspond to higher commissions regardless of the success of investment. Considering the naïve forecaster fallacy, an investment consultant would successively suggest the correct direction of a market in an increasing or decreasing trend and establish a reputation. When prices are very high, it may not be good timing for the investor, but it is pretty good timing for the consultant since commission is also very high. In the shipping business, we have many business activities set to commission-based fees. When freight rates and ship prices are very high, commissions also reach a peak, which gives incentive to every commission-based service provider to encourage investors to complete a transaction in the short term even if the timing is completely wrong.

The shipping industry is much more complex than is usually perceived. Awareness in such a complex environment is the most valuable asset and represents the highest level of asymmetric information. As well as providing newcomers with essential considerations to survive and prosper in the shipping business, I hope this book will improve your awareness and initiate some further discussion on various issues of the industry. There are so many topics that I did not mention specifically in this book, but another volume of the book may address those issues.

Note

1 http://news.bbc.co.uk/2/hi/business/8589042.stm, retrieved on April 15, 2018.

Appendix
Cognitive bias and logical fallacy

Do not trust yourself much

The roles of illusions, logical fallacies, and cognitive biases are greater than we previously thought. Our brains have quite a capacity for omission, ignorance, and overconfidence. I occasionally mentioned some of the issues in this book. Here, I will present them in a brief list for quick reference.

Self-serving bias

When we are successful, we believe it is the result of our own skills and efforts. When we fail, we blame external factors and do not believe the failure is our own fault.

Rationalization

How do we rationalize our failures? By using the rationalization features of our minds. We find some reason for the failure. It is a kind of false reasoning to eliminate the cognitive pain.

> Rationalization encourages irrational or unacceptable behavior, motives, or feelings and often involves ad hoc hypothesizing. This process ranges from fully conscious (e.g. to present an external defense against ridicule from others) to mostly subconscious (e.g. to create a block against internal feelings of guilt or shame).
>
> ('Rationalization (psychology)', 2018)

Optimism bias

We have a strong sense of our own perfection. We have a personal image of ourselves in a successful future. This motivates us and we position ourselves to seize the opportunities that will lead us to that future. However, such an outlook may blind our critical judgment.

Illusion of control and survivorship bias

Do you think you can control everything? No shipowner starts out to fail. Many thought that their spreadsheets were enough to secure the future of their investments. They thought they could control their assets and any outcomes. But a quick stroll through the cemetery of bankrupt shipping companies tells a different tale. Be aware of what you can control and what you cannot.

Planning fallacy

Our plans usually represent perfect conditions. They include no delays, problems, crises, or human errors. If this was normal, then why do we continually extend deadlines? Start with a bad scenario and have an adaptable plan. Make sure you budget in extra resources to cover the unexpected.

Confirmatory bias

We usually find a way to confirm our own ideas. To combat this natural tendency, we need some kind of robust falsification technique.

Hindsight bias

We frequently say, "I knew it!" If you really do know, then please tell me when the next downturn in the market will be. Some people have asymmetric knowledge, but that does not mean they have a crystal ball. We cannot know how things will move, but we can know the principles that drive them and be prepared for the big moves.

Gambler's fallacy

A historical peak is often followed by years of recession, but does it always work like that? At the beginning of 2005, we had a historical peak in the shipping markets, but then a few years afterward we had even more record highs.

Adaptation bias

Adaptation is one of the most powerful traits of mankind. However, people usually fail to anticipate the degree of adaptation required.

Winner's tragedy and overconfidence

Repetitive victories and successful business deals can be found throughout both market recoveries and peaks. Consecutive victories contribute to overconfidence and the optimism bias. This phenomenon is called the winner's tragedy or winner's effect.

Anchoring

People sometimes overvalue a piece of information when making their decision. They anchor their perspective on one trait and overlook other, contradictory sources of information.

Framing effect

Our knowledge sometimes depends on how we frame information. People draw different conclusions from the same information. The media uses news as a kind of framing effect. The format of information can easily change the perception of media consumers.

False dilemma

A false dilemma is a common logical fallacy in which people consider few alternatives when, in fact, others exist.

Hyperbolic discounting

Humans prefer rewards sooner rather than later. The cash flow of the short term is overvalued, while that of the far future is undervalued. The discounting rates of such calculations differ according to several factors, such as experience, the age of the decision-maker, etc.

False causality

When event A is followed by event B, then some people quickly deduce that A causes B. Causality is one of the hottest topics in the philosophy of science. David Hume presents the case that we can never be completely sure about a cause and effect relationship between events.

False correlation

Similar to false causality, people tend to see relationships between correlated (i.e. simultaneous) events. However, many variables may be highly correlated without there being an actual connection. With a trend data set, existing statistical methods can find spurious links between events. One should think critically about the underlying factors.

Appeal to authority

Some assume that a statement is correct because it was made by someone in authority. This is a fallacy because even experts' conclusions can be false.

Appeal to emotion

Others feel compelled to believe a statement is correct because it appeals to their emotions. That is, manipulative instruments are used to validate a statement without logical proof.

References

Adland, R. and Koekebakker, S., 2004. 'Market efficiency in the second-hand market for bulk ships.' *Maritime Economics & Logistics*, 6(1), 1–15.

Adland, R. and Strandenes, S., 2006. 'Market efficiency in the bulk freight market revisited.' *Maritime Policy & Management*, 33(2), 107–117.

Akerlof, G.A., 1978. 'The market for "lemons": Quality uncertainty and the market mechanism.' In P.A. Diamond and M. Rothschild (eds.), *Uncertainty in Economics*. New York: Academic Press, pp. 235–251.

Angier, E.A.V., 1920. *Fifty Years' Freights: 1869–1919*. London: Fairplay.

Beenstock, M. and Vergottis, A., 1993. *Econometric Modelling of World Shipping*. London: Chapman & Hall.

Benjamin, D.J., Berger, J.O., Johannesson, M., Nosek, B.A., Wagenmakers, E.J., Berk, R., Bollen, K.A., Brembs, B., Brown, L., Camerer, C. and Cesarini, D., 2018. 'Redefine statistical significance.' *Nature Human Behaviour*, 2(1), 6–10.

Bergius, W.C., 1871. 'On the commercial economy and performance of several types of merchant steamers on some of the principal lines of steam-ship traffic.' *Journal of the Society for Arts*, 19(959), 433–434.

Bernays, E.L., 1955. *The Engineering of Consent*. Norman, OK: University of Oklahoma Press.

Bouchaud, J.P., 2008. 'Economics needs a scientific revolution.' *Nature*, 455(7217), 1181.

Chang, H.J., 2014. *Economics: The User's Guide*. New York: Bloomsbury.

Charemza, W. and Gronicki, M., 1981. 'An econometric model of world shipping and shipbuilding.' *Maritime Policy & Management*, 8(1), 21–30.

Chen, M.K., 2013. 'The effect of language on economic behavior: Evidence from savings rates, health behaviors, and retirement assets.' *American Economic Review*, 103(2), 690–731.

Craig, R., 2003. *British Tramp Shipping, 1750–1914*, Research in Maritime History, No. 24. St. John's, Newfoundland: International Maritime Economic History Association.

Demyanyk, Y. and Van Hemert, O., 2009. 'Understanding the subprime mortgage crisis.' *The Review of Financial Studies*, 24(6), 1848–1880.

Duru, O., 2012. *Economic Analysis on the Long Term Assessment of Dry Bulk Shipping*. Doctoral dissertation, Kobe University, Japan.

Duru, O., 2013. 'Irrational exuberance, overconfidence and short-termism: Knowledge-to-action asymmetry in shipping asset management.' *The Asian Journal of Shipping & Logistics*, 29(1), 43–58.

Duru, O., 2014. 'Motivations behind irrationality in the shipping asset management: Assumptions drive investors.' The Conference of International Association of Maritime Economists, Norfolk, VA.

Duru, O., 2017. 'The origin and consistency of the ton-mile metric in the shipping economics.' *Logistics*, 1(1). doi:10.3390/logistics1010003.

Duru, O. and Yoshida, S., 2011. 'Long term freight market index and inferences.' *The Asian Journal of Shipping and Logistics*, 27(3), 405–421.

Eriksen, E.I., 1981. 'Demand for bulk ship services.' In E. Hope (ed.), *Studies in Shipping Economics: In Honour of Professor Arnljot Strømme Svendsen*. Oslo, Norway: Bedriftsøkonomens forlag, pp. 55–61

European Central Bank, 2013. Note: Comprehensive Assessment, December.

Fernando, V. (2009) 'Banks hide shipping losses with "the Hamburg Valuation"'. *Business Insider*, December 1. www.businessinsider.com/banks-try-to-hide-shipping-losses-with-the-hamburg-valuation-2009-12?IR=T.

Forrester, J., 1961. *Industrial Dynamics*. Waltham: Pegasus Communications.

Fox, N.R., 1994. 'An oligopoly model of ocean liner shipping.' *Review of Industrial Organization*, 9(3), 343–355.

George, R., 2013. *Ninety Percent of Everything: Inside Shipping, the Invisible Industry that Puts Clothes on Your Back, Gas in Your Car, and Food on Your Plate*. New York: Metropolitan.

Gerlach, M.L., 1992. *Alliance Capitalism: The Social Organization of Japanese Business*. Berkley, CA: University of California Press.

Gladwell, M., 2007. *Blink: The Power of Thinking Without Thinking*. New York: Back Bay Books.

Glen, D.R., 1997. 'The market for second-hand ships: Further results on efficiency using cointegration analysis.' *Maritime Policy and Management*, 24(3), 245–260.

Glen, D. and Martin, B., 2002. 'The tanker market: Current structure and economic analysis.' In C. Grammenos (ed.), *The Handbook of Maritime Economics and Business*. London: Lloyd's List, pp. 251–279.

Goleman, D., 1998. 'The emotional intelligence of leaders.' *Leader to Leader*, 1998 (10), 20–26.

Greenwood, R. and Hanson, S., 2013. *Waves in Ship Prices and Investment*, NBER Working Paper 19246. Cambridge, MA: National Bureau of Economic Research.

Harley, C.K., 1989. 'Coal exports and British shipping, 1850–1913.' *Explorations in Economic History*, 26(3), 311–338.

Huff, D., 1993. *How to Lie with Statistics*. New York: W.W. Norton.

International Monetary Fund, 2014. *Article IV Consultation—Staff Report; Press Release; And Statement By The Executive Director For Germany*, IMF Country Report No. 14/216, July 21. Washington, DC: IMF.

Kahneman, D., 2011. *Thinking, Fast and Slow*. London: Allen Lane.

Koekebakker, S. and Ådland, R., 2004. 'Modelling forward freight rate dynamics—empirical evidence from time charter rates.' *Maritime Policy & Management*, 31(4), 319–335.

Koekebakker, S., Adland, R. and Sødal, S., 2006. 'Are spot freight rates stationary?' *Journal of Transport Economics and Policy (JTEP)*, 40(3), 449–472.

Koopmans, T.C., 1939. *Tanker Freight Rates and Tankship Building: An Analysis of Cyclical Fluctuations*, Netherlands Economic Institute No. 27. Haarlem: F. Bohn.

LaRocco, L.A., 2012. *Dynasties of the Sea: The Shipowners and Financiers Who Expanded the Era of Free Trade*. Stamford, CT: Marine Money Inc.

Laverty, K.J., 1996. 'Economic "short-termism": The debate, the unresolved issues, and the implications for management practice and research.' *Academy of Management Review*, 21(3), 825–860.

Lo, A.W., 2011. *Fear, Greed, and Financial Crises: A Cognitive Neurosciences Perspective*, October 13. Available at SSRN: http://dx.doi.org/10.2139/ssrn.1943325.

Lo, A.W., 2017. *Adaptive Markets: Financial Evolution at the Speed of Thought*. Princeton, NJ: Princeton University Press.

Lorange, P., 2009. *Shipping Strategy: Innovating for Success*. Cambridge: Cambridge University Press.

Lun, Y.V., Lai, K.H. and Cheng, T.E., 2010. *Shipping and Logistics Management*. London: Springer.

McCleery, M., 2011. *The Shipping Man*. Stamford, CT: Marine Money International.

Metaxas, B.N., 1972. 'The future of the tramp shipping industry.' *Journal of Transport Economics and Policy*, 6(3), 271–280.

Moody's Investors Service, 2013. *German Shipping Lenders: Rising Problem Loans May Prompt Net Losses at Some Banks*, December 9. Available at: www.moodys.com.

Munshi, J., 2016. *Spurious Correlations in Time Series Data: A Note*. Available at SSRN: http://dx.doi.org/10.2139/ssrn.2827927.

North, D., 1958. 'Ocean freight rates and economic development 1730–1913.' *The Journal of Economic History*, 18(4), 537–555.

Paine, L., 2014. *The Sea and Civilization: A Maritime History of the World*. London: Atlantic Books.

Phelps Brown, H. and Hopkins, S.V., 1962. 'Seven centuries of prices of consumables, compared with builders' wage rates.' In E.M. Carus-Wilson (ed.), *Essays in Economic History, II*. London: Edward Arnold, pp. 179–196.

Porter, M.E. (1980) *Competitive Strategy, Techniques for Analysing Industries and Competitors*. New York: Free Press.

'Rationalization (psychology)', 2018. *Wikipedia*. Available at https://en.wikipedia.org/wiki/Rationalization_(psychology) (Accessed: 15 April 2018).

Reinhart, C.M. and Rogoff, K.S., 2009. *This Time is Different: Eight Centuries of Financial Folly*. Princeton, NJ: Princeton University Press.

Russell, B., 2001. *The Problems of Philosophy*. Oxford, Oxford University Press.

Sager, E.W. and Fischer, L.R., 1979. 'Patterns of investment in the shipping industries of Atlantic Canada, 1820–1900.' *Acadiensis*, 9(1), 19–43.

Sawers, L., 1992. 'The Navigation Acts revisited.' *The Economic History Review*, 45(2), 262–284.

Stanley, H.E., Amaral, L.A., Gabaix, X., Gopikrishnan, P. and Plerou, V., 2001. 'Similarities and differences between physics and economics.' *Physica A: Statistical Mechanics and its Applications*, 299(1–2), 1–15.

Stiglitz, J.E., 2009. 'The anatomy of a murder: Who killed America's economy?' *Critical Review*, 21(2–3), 329–339.

Stiglitz, J.E. and Weiss, A., 1981. 'Credit rationing in markets with imperfect information.' *The American Economic Review*, 71(3), 393–410.

Stopford, M., 2009. *Maritime Economics*. London: Routledge.

Sutcliffe, R.K., 2016. *British Expeditionary Warfare and the Defeat of Napoleon, 1793–1815*. Woodbridge, U.K.: Boydell & Brewer.

Sys, C., 2009. 'Is the container liner shipping industry an oligopoly?' *Transport Policy*, 16(5), 259–270.

Tinbergen, J., 1934. 'Tonnage and Freight.' *De Nederlandsche Conjunctuur*, March, 23–35. (Reprinted in J.H. Klassen, L.M. Koyck and H.J. Wittenveen (eds.), 1959. *Jan Tinbergen—Selected Papers*. Amsterdam: North Holland.)

Triana, P., 2011. *The Number that Killed Us: A Story of Modern Banking, Flawed Mathematics, and a Big Financial Crisis.* Hoboken, NJ: John Wiley & Sons.

Tvedt, J., 2003. 'Shipping market models and the specification of freight rate processes.' *Maritime Economics & Logistics*, 5(4), 327–346.

Veenstra, A.W., 1999. 'The term structure of ocean freight rates.' *Maritime Policy & Management*, 26(3), 279–293.

Walras, L., 1874. *Eléments d'économie politique pure ou théorie de la richesse sociale* (Elements of pure economics, or the theory of social wealth). Lausanne and Paris: L. Corbaz.

Wasserstein, R.L. and Lazar, N.A., 2016. 'The ASA's statement on *p*-values: Context, process, and purpose.' *The American Statistician*, 70(2), 129–133.

Woodlock, T.F., 1899. *Ton-Mile Cost*. New York: Dow Jones & Co.

Yasuba, Y., 1978. 'Freight rates and productivity in ocean transportation for Japan, 1875–1943.' *Explorations in Economic History*, 15(1), 11–39.

Index